Oxford Primary Writing Assessment

By Ros Wilson

OXFORD
UNIVERSITY PRESS

OXFORD
UNIVERSITY PRESS

Great Clarendon Street, Oxford, OX2 6DP,
United Kingdom

Oxford University Press is a department of the University of Oxford.
It furthers the University's objective of excellence in research, scholarship,
and education by publishing worldwide. Oxford is a registered trade mark of
Oxford University Press in the UK and in certain other countries.

Oxford Primary Writing Assessment © Oxford University Press 2015

This Edition published in 2015

The moral rights of the author have been asserted.

ISBN: 978-0-19-836719-2

1 3 5 7 9 10 8 6 4 2

Typset in Myriad Pro and FS Lola Primary

Paper used in the production of this book is a natural, recyclable product
made from wood grown in sustainable forests. The manufacturing process
conforms to the environmental regulations of the country of origin.

Printed and bound in Great Britain by Bell and Bain, Glasgow

Acknowledgements:

Oxford University Press would like to thank the following schools for their contribution
to the development and trialling of the Oxford Writing Criterion Scale:
Cravenwood Primary Academy, Crumpsall
Ludworth Primary School, Marple Bridge
Sir John Barrow Primary School, Ulverston
St. Bartholomew's C of E Primary School, Wiggington
Oldfields Hall Middle School, Uttoxeter
Aston Fields Middle School, Bromsgrove
Burchetts Green CE Infants School
Lowbrook Academy, Maidenhead

The following schools in Gloucestershire LA:
King's Stanley Primary School
Sherborne C of E Primary
Warden Hill Primary
Woodchester Endowed Primary
Harewood Juniors
Rodmarton Primary
Great Rissington Primary
Redbrooke Primary
Naunton Park Primary
Stroud Valley Community School
Mickleton Primary
Bledington CE Primary
Bibury Primary
Sheepscombe Primary
Haresfield Primary

Oxford Primary Writing Assessment

Contents

Introduction

Oxford Primary Reading Assessment provides comprehensive support for the teacher assessment of reading across a whole school.

The aim of this Handbook is to ensure that all children develop their full potential as writers by acquiring a wide range of writing skills and a life-long enthusiasm for writing. Together with its sister publication, *Oxford Primary Reading Assessment*, it provides schools with a whole school solution to teacher assessment of English, written by experts and thoroughly trialled in schools.

In this *Oxford Primary Writing Assessment* handbook, you will find:

- The **Oxford Writing Criterion Scale** – a comprehensive set of criteria created to inform consistent teacher assessment of writing from Reception/P1 right through to Year 6/P7

- Advice and simple tools to help teachers record and track pupil attainment and progress

- Clear next steps for children to ensure they make good progress

- Advice on reporting outcomes to parents and other stakeholders

- Exemplification of writing standards for each year group, with detailed commentary about judgements and next steps

- Additional writing samples for staff training and to support moderation

- A choice of writing 'starters' to use for summative assessment purposes.

Who is this book for?

All schools know that high quality assessment – linked to targeted and effective teaching – is the key to ensuring children make good progress. It allows teachers to identify and address any challenges children are facing as early as possible and also to extend and deepen learning for those who are ready.

For schools in England, the **Oxford Writing Criterion Scale** offers a comprehensive solution to assessment without Levels and can be used both as a periodic summative teacher assessment tool (see pages 8–9) and as a tool to inform next steps for success, both in the short and long term. It has been matched to the yearly expectations of the 2014 National Curriculum, so that teachers can assess, track and report pupil attainment and progress against these expectations. We have provided exemplification of the expected standard at the end of each year group as a guide.

Schools outside England, or those not following the National Curriculum in England, can also use the **Oxford Writing Criterion Scale** with confidence. That is because it based on a deep understanding of progression in writing and the skills children need to master along the way, and goes far beyond simply 'ticking the boxes' of the 2014 National Curriculum in England. The **Oxford Writing Criterion Scale** is a curriculum-neutral assessment tool that sets high expectations for all children and draws on best practice and expert subject knowledge.

About the Oxford Writing Criterion Scale

The Writing Criterion Scale was developed by assessment expert Ros Wilson. It describes the writing journey that children make, from their first pre-writing behaviours through to a more complex and sophisticated understanding and mastery of writing skills. The Writing Criterion Scale breaks down children's writing development into small steps so that it is easy to identify the point children have reached and the steps they need to make next in order to progress. Although the criteria are set out in a rough hierarchy, every child's writing journey is different, so the Writing Criterion Scale supports a 'best-fit' teacher judgement against national expectations whilst also giving teachers (and other stakeholders) a very accurate, individual picture for every child.

Developed over more than 15 years and informed by over 20,000 pieces of children's writing, the Writing Criterion Scale has recently undergone further development to ensure that it matches the expectations of the 2014 National Curriculum in England, and it is now known as the **Oxford Writing Criterion Scale**.

About the author

Ros Wilson

Ros Wilson has over forty-eight years' experience in education, including twenty-seven years in schools, ten years in Senior Management positions and fourteen years in advisory and inspection work. She has taught in primary, middle and secondary schools in England and overseas, and has wide experience in teaching and advising on raising achievement for pupils with English as an additional language and also pupils with special educational needs.

Ros has a Masters Degree in Education, specializing in assessment. As well as being the creator of the Writing Criterion Scale and the widely used *Big Writing* approach to raising standards in writing, she is also co-creator of the Reading Criterion Scale and the *Big Reading* programme.

The Oxford Writing Criterion Scale and Big Writing

It goes without saying that it is only through the effective teaching and development of children's writing skills that they will make the progress required. The Oxford Writing Criterion Scale can be used alongside any teaching approach but is particularly powerful when combined with *Big Writing*.

The *Big Writing* method has been proven over many years to be a highly effective approach to raising standards in writing. It focuses on:

1. Setting high expectations for all children and making writing fun!
2. Regular teaching and practice of basic skills (grammar, handwriting, spelling, punctuation)
3. Developing, through talk, the four key aspects of writing that make a real difference:
   - Vocabulary – increasingly ambitious words and phrases
   - Connectives – conjunctions, adverbs and prepositions to vary sentence structure
   - Openers – a range of techniques for opening sentences, again to vary structure
   - Punctuation – increasingly sophisticated forms of punctuation
4. Regular opportunities for children to apply their skills to extended writing
5. Ongoing assessment, marking and feedback of children's writing – by teachers and peers

If you would like to know more about Big Writing and the CPD offered visit www.andrelleducation.com

If you would like to know more about Oxford University Press' writing programme *Big Writing Adventures* visit www.oxfordprimary.co.uk

The Art of Writing

Writing is like ballet. It is only when all the steps have been learnt, the sequences have been rehearsed and re-rehearsed, the techniques have been honed and the performer has brought them all together in a wonderful interpretation of performance, that the abilities of the dancer (or the writer) can be truly judged. To know if a child has become a great writer we need to examine his or her actual writing, produced independently in response to a stimulus and purpose. The outcome of writing is 'the dance'.

The curriculum defines what skills and abilities a child should have learnt by the end of each year of primary education. Teachers, however, must know what the outcomes of that learning should look like if the child deploys that learning to maximum effect in a piece of unsupported writing. This is problematic as there are many factors that influence how successful a piece of writing is, including:

- the purpose of writing
- the type of text that would achieve that purpose
- the audience for the writing
- the stimulus for writing.

Add to this list the child's understanding and ability to select which of the myriad taught skills and abilities are the most appropriate and effective to achieve the maximum potential for achievement at or above age expectation, and we begin to understand the complexities of the task in hand.

Because it is such a complex skill, it is only when a child can consistently produce independent writing for a range of purposes and audiences around the expected standard for their age that they can be said to be writing securely at that standard.

Summative Assessment

Assessing the overall standard of achievement in writing through ongoing course work or work done in the course of daily practise is inappropriate for summative purposes. That type of assessment has a place – it is called formative assessment! It informs teaching and learning as the course progresses. At the end of the course, however, it is only by examining the individual's ability to use that learning to produce a unique work of art that we can judge the standard the individual is performing at.

Writing must be assessed through 'cold' performance – the child needs to draw on their long-term memory, which will be retained into the future, rather than their short-term memory, much of which may ultimately be forgotten. They must not have had immediate coaching or other input and should not be able to draw on information provided through scaffolds or classroom displays. The teaching has been done – we now need to know what the outcome is and what the child still truly needs to learn and what they need to do most urgently. Summative assessment of a child's writing should, therefore, take place termly to provide vital evidence of achievement.

Timing

Producing writing for assessment no longer needs to be time limited. Completion within a set time was necessary to prepare for an external testing system that no longer includes judgements on writing ability. It does, however, need to be done within one extended session, to ensure full independence. Alternative activities for 'brain breaks' might be provided if considered necessary, although by Upper Key Stage 2 roughly one hour to one and a quarter hours should be sufficient time to write, proof read, edit and improve a finished piece.

The only role for the teacher during production of the assessment piece might be quiet time prompts and monitoring that all the children seem comfortable and engaged.

Choosing appropriate stimuli for writing

Classes may be given a choice of three stimuli for the writing, from which they choose the one they feel most motivated by. It is, however, desirable that the whole key stage write to the same type of text. This enables better comparison of effectiveness of teaching, both of skills and of types of text.

Letters are a particularly useful text type for assessment purposes, particularly in the early stages, as they enable secure judgements on a wide range of features, such as organization and awareness of the audience. Particularly strong judgements are facilitated when the text is a 'hybrid', such as a letter with a set of embedded instructions, or a diary item or newspaper report.

Poetry, recount of a known story and narrative are not, usually, useful genres for assessment. Narrative is often the easiest and best context for developing writing skills, but children must be able to transfer their skills to at least two other text types before moving on. Otherwise they may use their writing voice in narrative only, where it is the obvious choice, and not in any other types of text, where it is essential for high level achievement.

For more suggestions of suitable tasks for the formal assessment of writing, see pages 76–77.

How to use the Oxford Writing Criterion Scale

The **Oxford Writing Criterion Scale** (OWCS) is designed to enable accurate, objective summative assessment of writing and to identify the next steps for a child in order for them to make progress.

The OWCS is organized into a series of Standards that map to the primary year groups, from Standard 1 (Reception/P1) through to Standard 7 (Year 6/P7).

Each Standard sets out a number of criteria against which children are assessed. The strands of writing that the criteria are assessing are:

- features of text type/genre
- handwriting
- spelling
- grammar
- punctuation
- writer's voice.

The OWCS and National Expectations

Assessments against each Standard result in a score which determines whether a child is **Developing**, **Secure** or **Advanced** against the expectations of their year group. Children should be judged as 'Secure' within a Standard by the end of each year in order to be tracking national expectations.

NOTE: By 'national expectations' we mean the aspirations of the 2014 National Curriculum. These aspirations are high and, at least in the short term, the required National Standard at the end of each key stage may well be lower. Schools in Scotland, Wales and Northern Ireland should refer to the appropriate curriculum correlation charts on pages 125–136.

Year Group	OWCS Assessment Standard	National Expectations by the end of the year
Reception/P1	Standard 1	Secure Standard 1
Year 1/P2	Standard 2	Secure Standard 2
Year 2/P3	Standard 3	Secure Standard 3
Year 3/P4	Standard 4	Secure Standard 4
Year 4/P5	Standard 5	Secure Standard 5
Year 5/P6	Standard 6	Secure Standard 6
Year 6/P7	Standard 7	Secure Standard 7

A very low score, usually below 6 points, means that a child is not yet working within that Standard and should be assessed against the Standard for the prior year group; a very high score – 2 or more points into the 'Advanced' category – prompts teachers to assess against the next Standard. Nevertheless, teachers will want to ensure children have mastered all the criteria in each Standard – and give children opportunities to deepen their understanding – before moving them on.

There is also a Pre-Writing Standard which sets out some very early writing behaviours and skills. Dependent on their pre-school experience, some children will have acquired the majority of these skills before entering Reception/P1 whilst others will need more help to develop the basics. The Pre-Writing Standard is designed to support an early baseline assessment of children's needs; those who tick most of the boxes can quickly be assessed and developed against Standard 1.

Making an Informed Assessment of a Child's Writing

When introducing the **Oxford Writing Criterion Scale**, most schools begin by conducting an initial or baseline summative assessment. It is recommended that a summative assessment is conducted once a term, e.g. in December, March and May/June, although some schools prefer a single 'end of year' assessment only.

Using the Oxford Writing Criterion Scale for summative assessment

As previously stated, it is vitally important that summative assessments are carried out on a piece of writing that is truly independent and unsupported and which, from Standard 2 onwards, is close to a side of A4 or more in length.

The summative assessment process is as follows:

Step	What to do	Notes
Step 1	Set an appropriate independent writing task for assessment purposes. You may want to offer children a choice of stimulus but it is important to ensure that every child is writing to the same text type.	*Further advice and ideas for writing tasks can be found on page 76*
Step 2	Select the appropriate OWCS Standard for the year group of the child, or children, you wish to assess.	*If you know, from other assessments or knowledge of a child, that a child is working well below expectations select the Standard from the prior year.*
Step 3	Photocopy a Standard for each child – adding their name and the date of the assessment.	
Step 4	Read through the piece of writing carefully. Then complete the OWCS using the following marks to indicate your judgement against each criterion: ✔ – there is clear, secure evidence in this piece that the child has mastered this skill ● – there is some evidence in this piece that the child can do this ✗ – there is no evidence in this piece that the child can do this (this could also indicate skills that have not been taught yet)	*You should expect to see three good examples to make a secure judgement although two particularly strong examples may be sufficient. At the higher Standards, one accurate and effective example of e.g. metaphor or the subjunctive would be acceptable.* *Remember: even if you think a child is secure or developing in a skill from previous work you must base your summative judgement on the evidence in this piece only.*
Step 5	Sometimes the text type or genre of the piece means that one or more criteria cannot be assessed. Each criterion that cannot be assessed should be marked with a dash [-].	
Step 6	Add up the number of ticks to generate a score and use the box at the bottom of the Standard to make a judgement.	*If one or more criteria are marked with a dash, reduce the points required to achieve each category accordingly. For example, if 'Developing' requires a score between 6-9 points it can be awarded for a score between 5-8 points if one criterion is unassessed or between 4-7 points if two criteria are unassessed.*
Step 7	If the piece of writing does not make the entry threshold for 'Developing' at the required Standard for the year group you should assess against the Standard for the prior year. If the piece of writing reaches an Assessment Point for a particular Standard you may assess against the Standard for the next year. However, if the piece does not meet the entry threshold for 'Developing' at the next Standard it should be recorded as 'Advanced' at the current Standard.	*This child will need focused support and intervention to help them make accelerated progress.* *You will want to ensure that this child has opportunities to broaden and deepen their skills within the Standard for their year group, as well as providing stretch in the form of new learning, as appropriate.*
Step 8	Children's basic skills – spelling, handwriting, punctuation – any 'essential skills' from the previous standard and those criteria marked with a ● can be used to inform the child's immediate next steps.	*For more information on next steps and target setting see page xx.*
Step 9	Retain the assessed piece of writing and the OWCS judgement in a class folder of evidence. Use a spreadsheet to record the pattern of assessments across the class over an academic year.	*An example class record is provided on page 13 and available electronically on Oxford Owl (www.oxfordowl.co.uk)*

An example of an OWCS assessment

Below is the summative assessment outcome of a piece of writing done by a Year 2/P3 child towards the end of the autumn term. The writer has been judged to be a Developing Standard 3 and is therefore on track to meet national expectations at the end of the year. Criteria marked with a ● indicate the most obvious next steps for this child. (For more information about target setting, see pages 50–55).

STANDARD 3: Year 2/P3

Name: Sam Peters   **Date:** 11/12/2014

No	Criteria	Evidence? (✔, ●, ✘)
1	Can communicate ideas and meaning confidently in a series of sentences of at least a paragraph in length. (May not be accurate, but mainly 'flows' as it has lost the 'list like' form typical of some early writing.)	✔
2	Can control use of ascenders/descenders and upper/lower case letters in handwriting.	✔
3	Can write in three or more text forms with reasonable accuracy. (If the writing is a narrative, simple report or recount of a known story, this cannot be ticked as they should already know these three text forms. If it is another genre, it can be ticked).	●
4	Can provide enough detail to interest the reader (e.g. is beginning to provide additional information or description beyond a simple list).	●
5	Can vary the structure of sentences to interest the reader (e.g. questions, direct speech or opening with a subordinate clause, etc.).	●
6	Can sometimes use interesting and ambitious words (they should be words not usually used by a child of that age, and not a technical word used in a taught context only, e.g. 'volcano' in geography or 'evaporate' in science).	✘
7	Can usually sustain narrative and non-narrative forms (can write at length – close to a side of A4 at least – staying on task).	✘
8	Can match organization to purpose (e.g. showing awareness of the structure of a letter, openings and endings, the importance of the reader, organizational devices, beginnings of paragraphing, etc.).	●
9	Can usually maintain the use of basic sentence punctuation (full stops followed by capital letters) in a piece close to a side of A4 in length. (May be on a shorter piece or may not be accurate to achieve the 'Developing' category.)	✔
10	Can spell most common words correctly and most of the Years R, 1 & 2 High Frequency Words, and the Year 1 & 2 words in the National Curriculum. Appendix 1.	●
11	Can use phonetically plausible strategies to spell or attempt to spell unknown polysyllabic words. (If all the spelling is correct in a long enough piece to provide secure evidence, tick this criterion.)	✔
12	Can use connectives other than 'and' to join two or more simple sentences, thoughts, ideas, etc. (e.g. but, so, then, or, when, if, that, because).	✔
13	Can use a range of punctuation, mainly correctly, including at least three of the following: full stop and capital letter, exclamation mark, question mark, comma (at least in lists), apostrophe for simple contraction and for singular possession (at least), e.g. 'John's dog...', 'The cat's bowl...'.	●
14	Can make their writing lively and interesting (e.g. provides additional detail, consciously uses humour, varies sentence length or uses punctuation to create effect, etc.).	✘
15	Can link ideas and events, using strategies to create 'flow' (e.g. Last time, also, after, then, soon, at last, and another thing . . .).	✘
16	Can use adjectives and descriptive phrases for detail and emphasis (consciously selects the adjective for purpose, rather than using a familiar one, e.g. a title: 'Big Billy Goat Gruff').	●
17	Structures basic sentences correctly, including capitals and full stops in a longer piece (one error is acceptable).	✔
18	Can use accurate and consistent handwriting (in print at a minimum, can show consistent use of upper/lower case, ascenders/descenders, size and form).	●
19	Begins to show evidence of joined handwriting.	✔
20	Uses past and present tenses correctly.	●
21	Can produce close to a side (or more) of A4 writing that is clear and coherent with one or more strong features	●
Total	Standard 3 – Developing	✔ = 8

Assessment score

0–5 ticks = Not yet working at this Standard; review against Standard 2
6–9 ticks = Developing
10–16 ticks = Secure
17–21 ticks = Advanced
Assessment point = Children with 18 or more ticks may be assessed against Standard 4.

Using the Oxford Writing Criterion Scale for formative assessment

For assessment to be effective in informing learning and leading to progress (the primary purpose of assessment, after all) it is important that it empowers children by giving them a very clear understanding of what they can do and what they need to do next to succeed.

The OWCS facilitates this by providing both a snapshot of a child's secure skills and evidence of the specific skills that are developing and/or need to be taught next in order for the child to make progress. The summative assessment will also flag up skills that really should be secure at a given point such as legible handwriting, accurate use of full stops and capital letters, or correct spelling of high frequency words. Teachers will want to focus on just two or three 'next steps' in setting individual targets for pupils and these targets can be shared with both pupils and parents. It is progress against these targets – and in spelling, handwriting and use of interesting vocabulary generally – that teachers need to focus on when marking children's writing between summative assessment points. These targets can be reviewed as progress is made.

Teachers will want to gather evidence of children applying and experimenting with new skills, and making progress against their targets, across a wide range of writing for different purposes, including different text types – and this is fine for formative assessment purposes. However, it is important to remember that only independent, unsupported writing should be used for summative assessment.

Further advice on target setting can be found on pages 50–55.

Tracking progress and ensuring mastery using the Oxford Writing Criterion Scale

It is the responsibility of every teacher to ensure children make progress in writing throughout the year and, with higher attainment targets and standards, the importance of being able to track and provide evidence of pupil progress cannot be understated. However, teachers need to be aware that progress in writing is not always about acquiring new skills and moving 'up'; depth and breadth of understanding and the ability to confidently apply knowledge and skills for a range of purposes and audiences is very important within a mastery curriculum.

The **OWCS** allows teachers to track both kinds of progress. At the summative assessment points children may move category – from developing to secure, for example – but should also increase their points score on the Standard for their year group. This means that, even if a child remains within the 'Developing' category between summative assessment points, teachers will be able to show progress in terms of points and against specific criteria as well as basic skills, as appropriate.

Within each category – **Developing**, **Secure** and **Advanced** – there will usually be a number of criteria against which children are not yet judged to be secure. Focusing on these as next steps for development – and indeed providing children with a range of opportunities to deepen their secure skills – will help teachers ensure mastery.

A simple Class Tracking Sheet for recording and tracking progress is provided on page 13 (and is available electronically on Oxford Owl.)

Further advice on tracking progress and reporting to different stakeholders can be found on pages 70–75.

Evidence of progress between summative assessments

Below is the summative assessment outcome of a piece of writing done by a Year 2/P3 child at the end of the spring term. It follows the assessment carried out in the autumn term – shown on page 10.

This child is now judged to be a Secure Standard 3 and should therefore be able to meet the National Standard in the end of Key Stage 1 teacher assessment. The child has made good progress from Developing to Secure and from a total of 8 to 13 points. However, there are still aspects of Standard 3 that this child needs to develop, in particular: varying sentence structure (on which no progress has been made), adding descriptive detail to interest the reader, and writing stamina in general.

STANDARD 3: Year 2/P3

Name: Sam Peters **Date:** 25/03/2015

No	Criteria	Evidence? (✔, ✗, ●)
1	Can communicate ideas and meaning confidently in a series of sentences of at least a paragraph in length. (May not be accurate, but mainly 'flows' as it has lost the 'list like' form typical of some early writing.)	✔
2	Can control use of ascenders/descenders and upper/lower case letters in handwriting.	✔
3	Can write in three or more text forms with reasonable accuracy. (If the writing is a narrative, simple report or recount of a known story, this cannot be ticked as they should already know these three text forms. If it is another genre, it can be ticked).	✔
4	Can provide enough detail to interest the reader (e.g. is beginning to provide additional information or description beyond a simple list).	✔
5	Can vary the structure of sentences to interest the reader (e.g. questions, direct speech or opening with a subordinate clause, etc.).	●
6	Can sometimes use interesting and ambitious words (they should be words not usually used by a child of that age, and not a technical word used in a taught context only, e.g. 'volcano' in geography or 'evaporate' in science).	✔
7	Can usually sustain narrative and non-narrative forms (can write at length – close to a side of A4 at least – staying on task).	✔
8	Can match organization to purpose (e.g. showing awareness of the structure of a letter, openings and endings, the importance of the reader, organizational devices, beginnings of paragraphing, etc.).	●
9	Can usually maintain the use of basic sentence punctuation (full stops followed by capital letters) in a piece close to a side of A4 in length. (May be on a shorter piece or may not be accurate to achieve the 'Developing' category.)	✔
10	Can spell most common words correctly and most of the Years R, 1 & 2 High Frequency Words, and the Year 1 & 2 words in the National Curriculum. Appendix 1.	✔
11	Can use phonetically plausible strategies to spell or attempt to spell unknown polysyllabic words. (If all the spelling is correct in a long enough piece to provide secure evidence, tick this criterion.)	✔
12	Can use connectives other than 'and' to join two or more simple sentences, thoughts, ideas, etc. (e.g. but, so, then, or, when, if, that, because).	●
13	Can use a range of punctuation, mainly correctly, including at least three of the following: full stop and capital letter, exclamation mark, question mark, comma (at least in lists), apostrophe for simple contraction and for singular possession (at least), e.g. 'John's dog...', 'The cat's bowl...'.	●
14	Can make their writing lively and interesting (e.g. provides additional detail, consciously uses humour, varies sentence length or uses punctuation to create effect, etc.).	✗
15	Can link ideas and events, using strategies to create 'flow' (e.g. Last time, also, after, then, soon, at last, and another thing...).	✗
16	Can use adjectives and descriptive phrases for detail and emphasis (consciously selects the adjective for purpose, rather than using a familiar one, e.g. a title: 'Big Billy Goat Gruff').	✔
17	Structures basic sentences correctly, including capitals and full stops in a longer piece (one error is acceptable).	✔
18	Can use accurate and consistent handwriting (in print at a minimum, can show consistent use of upper/lower case, ascenders/descenders, size and form).	✔
19	Begins to show evidence of joined handwriting.	✔
20	Uses past and present tenses correctly.	●
21	Can produce close to a side (or more) of A4 writing that is clear and coherent with one or more strong features	●
Total	Standard 3 – Secure	✔ = 13

Assessment score

0–5 ticks = Not yet working at this Standard; review against Standard 2 6–9 ticks = Developing 10–16 ticks = Secure	17–21 ticks = Advanced Assessment point = Children with 18 or more ticks may be assessed against Standard 4.

Oxford Writing Criterion Scale: Class progress tracking sheet

You may want to use a chart like this to record the headline judgements for each pupil on a termly basis. This provides a useful snapshot for top level analysis of the class.

A simple spreadsheet version of this chart is available online at Oxford Owl – see page 93 for details.

Year group and class:

Name	Date of birth	Autumn Term Assessment Date:		Spring Term Assessment Date:		Summer Term Assessment Date:	
		Judgement	Points	Judgement	Points	Judgement	Points
Example: Sam Peters	12/6/2008	3D	8	3S	13	3A	17
Example: Eloise Lodge	4/11/2007	2A	18	3D	6	3D	9

IMPORTANT NOTE: there is no standard number of 'points' progress required. The points score is merely indicative of general progress made against the OWCS.

Standardising and Moderating Writing Assessments

Assessing writing is a complex and often subjective process. The **Oxford Writing Criterion Scale** provides a common framework for assessment but cannot altogether eliminate difference of opinion between professionals. Developing a common – or 'standardised' – view of assessment judgements and holding regular moderation meetings will help to ensure the accuracy and consistency of assessments across a whole school.

It is also helpful to appoint an assessment lead; this may be the subject lead or someone experienced and confident in the assessment of writing. The assessment lead should be responsible for co-ordinating and managing the assessment process, leading the moderation meetings, gathering summative data and evidence and, as appropriate, working with the subject lead and senior management team to periodically review the schools' data.

An **Expanded Oxford Writing Criterion Scale** – with more detailed descriptions and exemplification for each criterion – is provided in Appendix 1 and can be used by new or less experienced staff in order to develop their subject knowledge and confidence in making judgements.

Six steps to standardisation

When the OWCS is first introduced to a school, the assessment lead should use the following process regularly (monthly if possible) to quickly build the confidence of all staff and create a standardised view of assessment judgements. The process takes about 15 minutes and should be carried out on a wide range of writing samples from across the year groups.

It is useful for the assessment lead to assess the piece of writing themselves, prior to the meeting, and to make notes on any aspects likely to cause debate or disagreement. This doesn't mean that the assessment lead comes with the 'right' answer; a collaborative process is important.

Step	What to do	Notes
1	Select a piece of unsupported, independent writing and remove the name of the child and any indication of their age or year group.	Removing the details of the child helps to avoid bias during the assessment process.
2	Place a copy of the piece (unassessed) on everyone's seat ahead of a staff meeting. Ask all staff to bring a copy of the Oxford Writing Criterion Scale to the meeting.	
3	Begin by asking everyone: Which Standard do you think this writing is at? Agree the Standard against which you will conduct the assessment.	Staff will quickly develop their instincts but initially this may need brief discussion.
4	Ask colleagues to spend just 5 minutes conducting the assessment, using Steps 4-6 of the process set out on page 9.	It is important the judgements are made fairly quickly and instinctively.
5	Spend a further 5 minutes discussing and agreeing a final judgement.	If in doubt, it is usually best to accept the harshest judgement given against a criterion. If there is not enough evidence for any one person to give a secure judgement, there is not enough evidence.
6	Finally, agree the 3 immediate next steps for the child.	Some difference of opinion is acceptable at this point.

Writing assessment moderation

Once teachers are confident in using the OWCS it is useful to meet occasionally as a whole staff to compare and moderate judgements and ensure the continued accuracy and consistency of writing assessment across the whole school.

The assessment lead should organise the moderation, which can follow the process for standardisation. However, during moderation meetings it is useful for teachers to work in small groups or pairs, assessing together and discussing their judgements before feeding back to the wider group.

Once agreement has been reached on the final judgement and immediate next steps, the assessment lead should file a dated copy of the piece of writing, the judgement and any notes or commentary. Over time, this will provide a comprehensive evidence base for future reference during moderation meetings so it is important to conduct the moderation assessments on a range of pieces across a range of Standards.

Children Working Below or Above Expectations (in England)

All schools and all classes will contain children from a range of backgrounds with a range of abilities. Background should never be a barrier to expectation or an excuse for low achievement but it may cause some children some difficulties along the way. The job of all teachers is to identify and address gaps as soon as they appear and to focus efforts on closing gaps as soon as possible. Assessment using the OWCS informs teachers of the precise nature of children's abilities to enable focused intervention – if required – or to suggest opportunities for development and stretch. By providing detailed evidence of exactly what a child can and can't do, the OWCS also supports communication between teachers and/or between schools at the vital transition points in a child's learning journey.

The Importance of Standards 2 and 3

Standards 2 and 3 of the OWCS contain almost all of the skills a child needs to demonstrate in order to be considered a writer, at the most basic level. Beyond this, the OWCS describes the increasing length, detail and sophistication of writing that children should demonstrate as they embed new vocabulary, new grammatical structures and new techniques, and as they mature.

It is therefore important to note:

- Children who are a Secure Standard 2 at the end of Year 1 are, theoretically, 'on track to meet national expectations' at the end of Key Stage 1. However, these children are not really secure or confident writers yet so the risk of them 'slipping back' remains high.

- Children who are still working at Standard 2 or who are a Developing Standard 3 at the end of Year 2 will fall short of the National Standard at the end of Key Stage 1 and are statistically very likely to fall short of National Standard at the end of Key Stage 2 (and on up to GCSE), unless they receive skilful intervention.

- Even children who are a Secure or an Advanced Standard 3 at the end of Year 2 are likely to have some aspects of their writing that still need development. The OWCS will help you to identify these.

- Almost all children in mainstream education who are said to have a special educational need in writing – either at Key Stage 2 or Key Stage 3 – are usually 'trapped' at some point between Standard 2 and Standard 3. They are not really writers and teaching at Key Stage 2 has moved on, without addressing their very early writing needs.

- Every teacher – in every year group – should know Standards 2 and 3 'inside out'. Teachers working at Key Stage 1 need to ensure that they firmly lay all the foundations a child needs to become a good writer whilst teachers at Key Stage 2 – and above – can rescue those who have fallen behind by focusing on these vital early skills.

Key Stage 2 expectations

By the end of Key Stage 2 all children should be consistently writing somewhere between Standard 6 and Standard 7. A child who is a Secure Standard 6 demonstrates all the knowledge and skills necessary to write with the competency of an adult and should achieve the National Standard in writing at the end of Key Stage 2.

It is important to note:

- Many children experience a 'dip' in performance at the transition between Key Stages, especially if this involves a change of setting, so even children who were judged to be 'Secure' or 'at National Standard' at the end of Key Stage 1 may have slipped back on entry to Key Stage 2. Continued teaching and practice of basic skills – and careful monitoring of assessments – is vital throughout Year 3/P4 and Year 4/P5 to ensure children retain and build upon the foundations laid in Key Stage 1.

- A child who is a Secure Standard 6 at the end of Key Stage 2 will be a competent writer and is likely to achieve National Standard in the key stage 2 teacher assessment. However, this child cannot be said to have 'mastered' all aspects of the primary curriculum and remains vulnerable to a 'dip' in performance in the transition to Key Stage 3.

- Children who are judged to be Developing at the Standard for their year group probably remain on track to reach National Standard at the end of Key Stage 2 but are vulnerable and should be monitored; further slippage should be addressed immediately.

- Progress can be more erratic at Key Stage 2 as children are required to write for an increasing range of purposes and audiences and demonstrate knowledge from the wider curriculum. Careful monitoring of a range of children's writing together with the summative assessments will help you identify 'blips' versus 'trends'.

- Children who are judged to be Advanced at the Standard for their year group will continue to have aspects of their writing that need development and should be encouraged to broaden and deepen their secure skills in a range of contexts.

- Standard 7 includes some of the more sophisticated aspects of grammar found in the primary curriculum but otherwise describes progress related entirely to increasing length and maturity of content. Children who are a Secure Standard 7 when they leave primary school are well placed to meet the demands of the secondary curriculum. Progress for these children will be about communicating increasingly sophisticated knowledge in increasingly challenging and complex contexts.

The **Oxford** Writing Criterion Scale

Developed by Ros Wilson

Pre-Writing Standard: Early Years

The Pre-Writing Standard supports the observation and recording of early writing behaviours and oral language skills. It is designed to help teachers evaluate children's pre-school experiences so that they can best meet the needs of the whole class. It is not designed as a summative assessment tool.

Children whose experience of talk, writing and language is good prior to starting school will readily demonstrate many of these behaviours and you will be able to teach, observe and assess these children against 'Standard 1' fairly quickly. Other children will need more exposure to language and early motor skills before they are ready for the more formal teaching of writing to begin.

PRE-WRITING STANDARD: Early Years

Name: Date:

No	Criteria	Evidence? (✔, ✗, ●)
1	Will tolerate hand manipulation.	
2	Will work with another to allow mark-making using body parts or an implement.	
3	Will attempt to mark-make independently.	
4	Can recognize mark-making materials.	
5	Can use and enjoys mark-making materials.	
6	Can show some control in mark-making.	
7	Can produce some recognizable letters.	
8	Can differentiate between different letters and symbols.	
9	Shows some awareness of the sequencing of letters.	
10	Can copy over/under a model.	
11	Can imitate adults' writing and understands the purpose of writing.	
12	Can name three or more different purposes of writing.	
13	Can ascribe meaning to own mark-making ('reads' what has been 'written').	
14	Knows print has meaning and that, in English, it is read from left to right and top to bottom.	
15	Can write the initial letter of their own name.	
16	Can attempt to 'write' things, including their own name, using random letters.	
17	Can write their own name, although it may be with wrong letter formations or mixed lower/upper case.	
18	Can recognize their own first name when it is written in clear print.	

Standard 1: Reception/P1

Standard 1 can be used both for the termly formal assessment of children's writing throughout Year 1/P2 and to identify the next steps required for progress.

Essential Pre-Writing skills

Before being assessed against Standard 1, children must be beginning to:

- Draw identifiable letters and/or write his/her own name.

Standard 1: Reception/P1 – end of year expectation

By the end of the Reception Year, children should be able to:

- Write three or more simple statements on a given subject that can be read without the child's help and that make sense, although letter shapes and spelling may not be fully accurate. There may be no full stops (or there may be one or more in the wrong places) and use of capitals and lower case letters may not be fully established.

Children are expected to be a 'Secure Standard 1' by the end of the Reception Year in order to be on track to meet National Expectations at the end of KS1.

NOTE: Children moving up into Year 1/P2 who have not achieved against criteria 18 and 19 from Standard 1 must focus on these as a priority.

Standard 1: Reception/P1

Name: Date:

No	Criteria (listed in an approximate hierarchy)	Evidence? (✔, ✗, ●)
1	Can draw recognizable letters of the alphabet.	
2	Can write their own name.	
3	Can 'write' things using a mix of appropriate and random letters.	
4	Can sequence most of the letters of the alphabet.	
5	Can write their own name with the correct letter formations, although the size and shape may be slightly inconsistent.	
6	Can name the purpose of different texts/types of writing (at least three).	
7	Can 'read' what he/she has 'written'.	
8	Can hold and use a pencil effectively.	
9	Can spell some of the words from the Year R High Frequency Word list.	
10	Can spell CVC (consonant, vowel, consonant) words (e.g. sit, bag, cat) usually correctly.	
11	Can write simple labels and captions.	
12	Can usually leave a space between emerging words.	
13	Can show some control over word order, producing short logical statements, trying to use emergent phonics for spellings not known.	
14	Can produce two or more logical statements on the same subject.	
15	Can spell many words on the Year R High Frequency Word list.	
16	Is beginning to attempt to write simple known stories.	
17	Can say what they want to write, speaking in clearly defined statements or sentences.	
18	Can spell many common, single syllable words correctly in writing, including most of the words in the Year R High Frequency Word list and the Early Years Outcomes.	
19	Can write three or more simple statements on a given subject that can be read without the child's help and that make sense, although letter shapes and spelling may not be fully accurate.	

Assessment score

0–2 ticks = not yet working at this Standard; review against Pre-Writing Standard.
3–8 ticks = Developing
9–16 ticks = Secure
17–19 ticks = Advanced
Assessment point: children with 18 or more ticks may be assessed against Standard 2.

Standard 2: Year 1/P2

Standard 2 can be used both for the termly formal assessment of children's writing throughout Year 1/P2 and to identify the next steps required for progress.

Essential Standard 1 skills

The following skills must be secured as quickly as possible in Year 1/P2:

- Write three or more simple statements on a given subject that can be read without the child's help and that make sense, although letter shapes and spelling may not be fully accurate. There may be no full stops (or there may be one or more in the wrong places) and use of capitals and lower case letters may not be fully established.

Standard 2: Year 1/P2 – end of year expectation

By the end of Year 1/P2, children should be able to:

- Produce a paragraph or more of developed ideas independently that can be read without help from the child. The outcome may be more like spoken than written language but must not be a retelling.

- Write one or more sentences extended by the use of 'and' or another conjunction and two or more sentences showing the correct use of full stops and capital letters.

- Usually spell most CVC words and most common words from the Reception and Year 1 Word lists correctly.

- Produce letter shapes which are mainly accurate, with clear spaces between most words.

Children are expected to be a 'Secure Standard 2' by the end of Year 1 in order to be on track to meet national expectations at the end of KS1.

STANDARD 2: Year 1/P2

Name: Date:

No	Criteria	Evidence? (✔, ✗, ●)
1	Can write their own first name with appropriate upper and lower case letters (may not be totally accurate).	
2	Can form all letters clearly, although size and shape may be irregular.	
3	Writes simple regular words, some spelt correctly.	
4	Almost always leaves spaces between words.	
5	Makes sensible phonic attempts at words.	
6	Can spell all CVC (consonant, vowel, consonant) words (e.g. sit, bag, cat) correctly.	
7	Confidently writes some captions and labels and attempts other simple forms of writing (e.g. lists, stories, retellings etc.).	
8	Can show some control over letter size, shape and orientation in writing.	
9	Can say what their writing says and means.	
10	Can retell known stories in writing.	
11	Can produce their own ideas for writing (not a retelling).	
12	Can show some control over word order, producing logical statements.	
13	Can spell most of the Year R and 1 High Frequency Words and the Year 1 words in the National Curriculum. Appendix 1.	
14	Can make recognizable attempts at spelling words not known (almost all decodable without the child's help). (If all are spelt correctly, tick this criterion so as not to penalize the child).	
15	Can write simple texts such as lists, stories, reports, recounts (of a paragraph or more).	
16	Begins to show awareness of how full stops are used in writing. (May be in the wrong places or only one, final full stop.)	
17	Can usually give letters a clear and regular size, shape and orientation (ascenders and descenders and use of upper and lower case are usually accurate).	
18	Can use ANY connective (may only ever be 'and') to join two simple sentences, thoughts, ideas, etc.	
19	Can use appropriate vocabulary (should be coherent and sensible) in more than three statements.	
20	Can always use logical phonic strategies when trying to spell unknown words in more than three statements.	
21	Can usually use a capital letter and full stop, question mark or exclamation mark to punctuate sentences.	
22	Can produce a paragraph or more of developed ideas independently that can be read without help from the child (may be more like spoken than written language but must not be a retelling).	

Assessment score

0–6 ticks = not yet working at this Standard; review against Standard 1.
7–12 ticks = Developing
13–17 ticks = Secure
18–22 ticks = Advanced
Assessment point: children with 20 or more ticks may be assessed against Standard 3.

Standard 3: Year 2/P3

Standard 3 can be used both for the termly formal assessment of children's writing throughout Year 2/P3 and to identify the next steps required for progress.

Essential Standard 2 skills

The following skills must be secured as a priority in Year 2/P3:

- Produce a paragraph or more of developed ideas independently that can be read without help from the child. The outcome may be more like spoken than written language but must not be a retelling.

- Write one or more sentences extended by the use of 'and' or another conjunction and two or more sentences showing the correct use of full stops and capital letters.

- Usually spell most CVC words and most common words from the Reception and Year 1 word lists correctly.

- Produce letter shapes which are mainly accurate, with clear spaces between most words.

Standard 3: Year 2/P3 – end of year expectation

By the end of Year 2/P3, children should be able to:

- Produce close to a side (or more) of A4 writing that is clear and coherent with one or more strong features, responding mainly correctly to stimulus and purpose (not in a retelling, narrative or poem).

- Write sentences which show some variety, at least in the words with which they open, and which include some descriptive language and/or detail, including adjectives, adverbs and associated expanded phrases.

- Use some ambitious words for their age (occasional misuse is acceptable).

- Spell all CVC and most common words on the Year R, 1 and 2 word lists correctly, plus most simple compound words. Spelling of unknown complex words should be phonetically logical.

- Use simple past and present tenses mainly correctly.

- Correctly use three or more different connectives and three or more different types of punctuation, with most sentences demarcated with final punctuation followed by a capital letter.

- Produce handwriting which is controlled, mainly regular in size and becoming neat. There may be evidence of joining.

Children are expected to be a 'Secure Standard 3' by the end of Year 2 in order to be on track to meet national expectations at the end of KS1.

STANDARD 3: Year 2/P3

Name: Date:

No	Criteria	Evidence? (✔, ✗, ●)
1	Can communicate ideas and meaning confidently in a series of sentences of at least a paragraph in length. (May not be accurate, but mainly 'flows' as it has lost the 'list like' form typical of some early writing.)	
2	Can control use of ascenders/descenders and upper/lower case letters in handwriting.	
3	Can write in three or more text forms with reasonable accuracy. (If the writing is a narrative, simple report or recount of a known story, this cannot be ticked as they should already know these three text forms. If it is another genre, it can be ticked).	
4	Can provide enough detail to interest the reader (e.g. is beginning to provide additional information or description beyond a simple list).	
5	Can vary the structure of sentences to interest the reader (e.g. questions, direct speech or opening with a subordinate clause, etc.).	
6	Can sometimes use interesting and ambitious words (they should be words not usually used by a child of that age, and not a technical word used in a taught context only, e.g. 'volcano' in geography or 'evaporate' in science).	
7	Can usually sustain narrative and non-narrative forms (can write at length – close to a side of A4 at least – staying on task).	
8	Can match organization to purpose (e.g. showing awareness of the structure of a letter, openings and endings, the importance of the reader, organizational devices, beginnings of paragraphing, etc.).	
9	Can usually maintain the use of basic sentence punctuation (full stops followed by capital letters) in a piece close to a side of A4 in length. (May be on a shorter piece or may not be accurate to achieve the 'Developing' category.)	
10	Can spell most common words correctly and most of the Years R, 1 & 2 High Frequency Words, and the Year 1 & 2 words in the National Curriculum Appendix 1.	
11	Can use phonetically plausible strategies to spell or attempt to spell unknown polysyllabic words. (If all the spelling is correct in a long enough piece to provide secure evidence, tick this criterion.)	
12	Can use connectives other than 'and' to join two or more simple sentences, thoughts, ideas, etc. (e.g. but, so, then, or, when, if, that, because).	
13	Can use a range of punctuation, mainly correctly, including at least three of the following: full stop and capital letter, exclamation mark, question mark, comma (at least in lists), apostrophe for simple contraction and for singular possession (at least), e.g. 'John's dog...', 'The cat's bowl....'	
14	Can make their writing lively and interesting (e.g. provides additional detail, consciously uses humour, varies sentence length or uses punctuation to create effect, etc.).	
15	Can link ideas and events, using strategies to create 'flow' (e.g. Last time, also, after, then, soon, at last, and another thing...).	
16	Can use adjectives and descriptive phrases for detail and emphasis (consciously selects the adjective for purpose, rather than using a familiar one, e.g. a title: 'Big Billy Goat Gruff').	
17	Structures basic sentences correctly, including capitals and full stops in a longer piece (one error is acceptable).	
18	Can use accurate and consistent handwriting (in print at a minimum, can show consistent use of upper/lower case, ascenders/descenders, size and form).	
19	Begins to show evidence of joined handwriting.	
20	Uses past and present tenses correctly.	
21	Can produce close to a side (or more) of A4 writing that is clear and coherent with one or more strong features.	

Assessment score

0–5 ticks = not yet working at this Standard; review against Standard 2
6–9 ticks = Developing
10–16 ticks = Secure
17–21 ticks = Advanced
Assessment point: children with 18 or more ticks may be assessed against Standard 4.

Standard 4: Year 3/P4

Standard 4 can be used both for the termly formal assessment of children's writing throughout Year 3 and to identify the next steps required for progress.

Essential Standard 3 skills

The following skills must be secured as a priority in Year 3/P4:

- Produce close to a side (or more) of A4 writing that is clear and coherent with one or more strong features, responding mainly correctly to stimulus and purpose (not in a retelling, narrative or poem).

- Write sentences which show some variety, at least in the words with which they open, and which include some descriptive language and/or detail, including adjectives, adverbs and associated expanded phrases.

- Use some ambitious words for their age (occasional misuse or 'purple prose' is acceptable).

- Spell all CVC and most common words on the Year R, 1 and 2 word lists correctly, plus most simple compound words. Spelling of unknown complex words should be phonetically logical.

- Use simple past and present tenses mainly correctly.

- Correctly use three or more different connectives and three or more different types of punctuation, with most sentences demarcated with final punctuation followed by a capital letter.

- Produce handwriting which is controlled, mainly regular in size and becoming neat. There may be evidence of joining.

Standard 4: Year 3/P4 – end of year expectation

By the end of Year 3/P4, children should be able to:

- Produce close to a side or more of A4 writing that is clear and coherent with some of the features below.

- Interpret the stimulus and purpose broadly accurately and demonstrate about 75% accuracy in basic skills.

- Show variety in sentence structure, including opening in a range of ways, adding detail and/or description and using a wider range of connectives and punctuation.

- Use interesting language with some use of words that are ambitious for their age (occasional misuse or 'purple prose' is acceptable).

- Use most past and present tense verbs accurately.

- Begin to use direct speech and a wider range of connectives (conjunctions, adverbs and prepositions) to show time, place and cause.

- Begin to use paragraphs.

- Produce handwriting that is neat and mainly joined.

- Initiate edits and improvements to their work by proof reading what they have written.

Children are expected to be a 'Secure Standard 4' by the end of Year 3 in order to be on track to meet national expectations at the end of KS2.

STANDARD 4: Year 3/P4

Name: Date:

No	Criteria	Evidence? (✔, ✗, ●)
1	Can produce work which is organized, imaginative and clear (e.g. simple opening and ending).	
2	Can usually join their handwriting.	
3	Can use a range of chosen forms appropriately and consistently. (If the writing is a narrative, simple report or recount of a known story, this cannot be ticked. If it is another genre, it can be ticked).	
4	Can adapt their chosen form to the audience (e.g. provide information about characters or setting, make a series of points, use brackets for asides, etc.).	
5	Can sometimes use interesting and ambitious words (they should be words not usually used by a child of that age, and not a technical word used in a taught context only, e.g. 'volcano' in geography or 'evaporate' in science).	
6	Can develop and extend ideas logically in sequenced sentences (but they may still be overly detailed or brief).	
7	Can extend sentences using a wider range of connectives to clarify relationships between points and ideas (e.g. when, because, if, after, while, also, as well).	
8	Can usually use correct grammatical structures in sentences (nouns and verbs generally agree).	
9	Can use pronouns appropriately to avoid the awkward repetition of nouns.	
10	Can use most punctuation accurately, including at least three of the following: full stop and capital letter, question mark, exclamation mark, comma, apostrophe.	
11	Can structure and organize work clearly (e.g. beginning, middle, end; letter structure; dialogue structure).	
12	Is beginning to use paragraphs.	
13	Can adapt form and style for purpose (e.g. there is a clear difference between formal and informal letters; use of abbreviated sentences in notes and diaries, etc.).	
14	Can write neatly, legibly and accurately, mainly in a joined style.	
15	Can use adjectives and adverbs for description.	
16	Can spell phonetically regular or familiar common polysyllabic words accurately (sometimes for the 'Developing' category) and most or all of the Year 3 High Frequency Words and the Year 3 words in the National Curriculum Appendix 1.	
17	Can develop characters and describe settings, feelings and/or emotions, etc.	
18	Can link and relate events, including past, present and future, sensibly (afterwards, before, also, after a while, eventually, etc)	
19	Can attempt to give opinion, interest or humour through detail.	
20	Can use generalizing words for style (e.g. sometimes, never, always, often, mainly, mostly, generally, etc.) and/or modal verbs/ the conditional tense (e.g. might do it, may go, could rain, should win).	
21	Is beginning to develop a sense of pace (writing is lively and interesting).	

Assessment score

0–5 ticks = not yet working at this Standard; review against Standard 3.
6–9 ticks = Developing
10–17 ticks = Secure
18–21 ticks = Advanced
Assessment point: children with 19 or more ticks may be assessed against Standard 5.

Standard 5: Year 4/P5

Standard 5 can be used both for the termly formal assessment of children's writing throughout Year 4/P5 and to identify the next steps required for progress.

Essential Standard 4 skills

The following skills must be secured as a priority in Year 4/P5:

- Produce close to a side or more of A4 writing that is clear and coherent with some of the features below.

- Interpret the stimulus and purpose broadly accurately and demonstrate about 75% accuracy in basic skills.

- Show variety in sentence structure, including opening in a range of ways, adding detail and/or description and using a wider range of connectives and punctuation.

- Use interesting language with some use of words that are ambitious for their age (occasional misuse or 'purple prose' is acceptable).

- Use most past and present tense verbs accurately.

- Begin to use direct speech and a wider range of connectives (conjunctions, adverbs and prepositions) to show time, place and cause.

- Begin to use paragraphs.

- Produce handwriting that is neat and mainly joined.

- Initiate edits and improvements to their work by proof reading what they have written.

Standard 5: Year 4/P5 – end of year expectation

By the end of Year 4/P5, children should be able to:

- Produce more than a side of A4 writing that is clear and coherent with strong features and accurate interpretation of the stimulus and purpose.

- Spell most common words on the Year 3 and 4 word lists correctly, plus all compound words and many complex words.

- Show variety in sentence type and structure, including more sophisticated sentence opening, adding detail and/or description and using a wider range of sophisticated connectives.

- Use interesting language with a wide range of words that are ambitious for their age (occasional misuse is acceptable).

- Use a wide range of punctuation accurately.

- Use a wider range of connectives (conjunctions, adverbs and prepositions) to show time, place and cause.

- Produce handwriting that is neat and joined.

- Organize writing appropriately for the purpose, including using paragraphs.

- Initiate edits and improvements to their work by proof reading what they have written.

Children are expected to be a 'Secure Standard 5' by the end of Year 4 in order to be on track to meet national expectations at the end of KS2.

STANDARD 5: Year 4/P5

Name: Date:

No	Criteria	Evidence? (✔, ✗, ●)
1	Can write in a lively and coherent style.	
2	Can use a range of styles and genres confidently and independently. (If the writing is a narrative, simple report or recount of a known story this cannot be ticked. If any other genre, it can be ticked as they will already know these three text forms.)	
3	Can sometimes use interesting and ambitious words (they should be words not usually used by a child of that age, and not a technical word used in a taught context only, e.g.' volcano' in geography or 'evaporate' in science).	
4	Can organize ideas appropriately for both purpose and reader (e.g. captions, headings, bullets, fonts, chapters, letter formats, paragraphs, logically sequenced events, contextual and background information etc.).	
5	Can use a wide range of punctuation mainly accurately, including at least three of the following: full stop and capital letter, question mark, exclamation mark, apostrophe and comma.	
6	Can write neatly, legibly and accurately, usually maintaining a joined style.	
7	Can use more sophisticated connectives (e.g. although, however, nevertheless, despite, contrary to, as well as, etc.).	
8	Can use links to show time and cause.	
9	Can open sentences in a wide range of ways for interest and impact.	
10	Can use paragraphs, although they may not always be accurate.	
11	Can produce thoughtful and considered writing (uses simple explanation, opinion, justification and deduction).	
12	Can use or attempt grammatically complex structures (e.g. expansion before and after the noun: 'The little, old man who lived on the hill...', '... by the lady who taught me the guitar...'; subordinate clauses: 'I felt better when...', etc.).	
13	Can spell unfamiliar regular polysyllabic words accurately and most or all of the Year 4 High Frequency Words and the Year 4 words in the National Curriculum. Appendix 1.	
14	Can use nouns, pronouns and tenses accurately and consistently throughout.	
15	Can use apostrophes and/or inverted commas, mainly accurately. (If direct speech is not appropriate to the task, apostrophes alone can score the tick).	
16	Can select from a range of known adventurous vocabulary for a purpose, with some words being particularly well chosen.	
17	Can select interesting strategies to move a piece of writing forward (e.g. asides, characterization, dialogue with the audience, dialogue, etc.).	
18	Can advise assertively, although not confrontationally, in factual writing (e.g. 'An important thing to think about before deciding...', 'We always need to think about...', etc.).	
19	Can develop ideas in creative and interesting ways.	

Assessment score

0–5 ticks = not yet working at this Standard; review against Standard 4.
6–9 ticks = Developing
10–15 ticks = Secure
16–19 ticks = Advanced
Assessment point: children with 17 or more ticks may be assessed against Standard 6.

Standard 6: Year 5/P6

Standard 6 can be used both for the termly formal assessment of children's writing throughout Year 5/P6 and to identify the next steps required for progress.

Essential Standard 5 skills

The following skills must be secured as a priority in Year 5/P6:

- Produce more than a side of A4 writing that is clear and coherent with strong features and accurate interpretation of the stimulus and purpose.

- Spell most common words on the Year 3 and 4 word lists correctly, plus all compound words and many complex words.

- Show variety in sentence type and structure, including more sophisticated openings, adding detail and/or description and using a wider range of sophisticated connectives.

- Use interesting language with a wide range of words that are ambitious for their age (occasional misuse is acceptable).

- Use a wide range of punctuation accurately.

- Use a wider range of connectives (conjunctions, adverbs and prepositions) to show time, place and cause.

- Produce handwriting that is neat and joined.

- Organize writing appropriately for the purpose, including using paragraphs.

- Initiate edits and improvements to their work by proof reading what they have written.

Standard 6: Year 5/P6 – end of year expectation

By the end of Year 5/P6, children should be able to:

- Show variety in sentence type and structure, including the confident use of a range of sentence openings, punctuation for effect and the inclusion of additional detail and/or description.

- Use very interesting language with a wide range of words that are ambitious for their age and some literary features (e.g. alliteration, onomatopoeia, figurative language, etc.).

- Use the full range of punctuation accurately (as and when appropriate).

- Use a range of formal and informal styles or 'voice' when appropriate.

- Use a wide range of connectives for the full range of purposes and begin to use more sophisticated connectives.

- Produce handwriting that is fluent, neat and joined.

- Organize writing appropriately, including the use of paragraphs and a range of organizational devices.

- Initiate edits and improvements to their work by proof reading what they have written.

Children are expected to be a 'Secure Standard 6' by the end of Year 5 in order to be on track to meet national expectations at the end of KS2.

STANDARD 6: Year 5/P6

Name: Date:

No	Criteria	Evidence? (✔, ✗, ●)
1	Can produce well-structured and organized writing using a range of conventions in layout.	
2	Can use appropriate informal and formal styles with confidence (e.g. conversational, colloquial, dialect, Standard English).	
3	Can select the correct genre for audience and purpose, and use it accurately.	
4	Can select from a wide range of known imaginative and ambitious vocabulary (they should be words that are not usually used by a child of that age) and use them precisely. (All spelling, including that of complex words, is almost always correct.)	
5	Can use paragraphs consistently and appropriately.	
6	Can group things appropriately before or after a main verb (e.g. 'The books, the pens and the pencils were all ready on the table').	
7	Can use all grammar accurately except when consciously using dialect or colloquialism for purpose and audience.	
8	Can use different techniques to open or conclude work appropriately (e.g. opinion, summary, justification, comment, suspense or prediction).	
9	Can use complex sentence structures appropriately.	
10	Can use a wider range of punctuation, almost always accurately, to include three or more of the following (as appropriate to the text): comma, apostrophe, bullets, inverted commas, hyphen, brackets, colon or semi-colon.	
11	Can use punctuation appropriately to create effect (e.g. exclamation mark, dash, question mark, ellipsis).	
12	Can write neatly, legibly and accurately in a flowing, joined style.	
13	Can adapt handwriting for a range of tasks and purposes, including for effect.	
14	Can spell accurately in all but the most complex words (e.g. paraphernalia, quintessential etc.) and most or all of the Year 5 High Frequency Words and the Year 5 words in the National Curriculum Appendix 1.	
15	Can use the passive voice for variety and to shift focus (e.g. 'The cake was eaten by the child').	
16	Can use a range of narrative techniques with confidence, interweaving elements when appropriate (e.g. action, dialogue, quotation, formal or informal style, aside, observation, suspense).	
17	Can vary sentence length and word order confidently to sustain interest (e.g. 'Having achieved your goals at such an early age, what motivates you to continue? Why fight on?').	
18	Can use a range of devices to adapt writing to the needs of the reader (e.g. headings, sub-headings, bullets, underlining, parenthesis, introduction providing context, footnote, contents, bibliography).	
19	Can use literary features to create effect (e.g. alliteration, onomatopoeia, figurative language, dialect, metaphor, simile etc.).	
20	Can interweave implicit and explicit links between sections.	
21	Can use punctuation to show division between clauses, to indicate, to vary pace, to create atmosphere or to sub-divide (e.g. commas, colons, semicolons, dashes, ellipses).	
22	Can show confident and established 'voice'.	

Assessment score

0–7 ticks = not yet working at this Standard; review against Standard 5.
8–11 ticks = Developing
12–18 ticks = Secure
19–22 ticks = Advanced
Assessment point: children with 20 or may ticks may be assessed against Standard 7.

Standard 7: Year 6/P7

Standard 7 can be used both for the termly formal assessment of children's writing throughout Year 6/P7 and to identify the next steps required for progress.

Essential Standard 6 skills

The following skills must be secured as a priority in Year 6/P7:

- Show variety in sentence type and structure, including the confident use of a range of sentence openings, punctuation for effect and the inclusion of additional detail and/or description.

- Use very interesting language with a wide range of words that are ambitious for their age and some literary features (e.g. alliteration, onomatopoeia, figurative language, etc.).

- Use the full range of punctuation accurately (as and when appropriate).

- Use a range of formal and informal styles or 'voice' when appropriate.

- Use a wide range of connectives for the full range of purposes and begin to use more sophisticated connectives.

- Produce handwriting that is fluent, neat and joined.

- Organize writing appropriately, including the use of paragraphs and a range of organizational devices.

- Initiate edits and improvements to their work by proof reading what they have written.

Children are expected to be a 'Secure Standard 6' by the end of Year 5 in order to be on track to meet national expectations at the end of KS2.

Standard 7: Year 6/P7 – end of year expectation

By the end of Year 6/P7, children should be able to:

- demonstrate a wide range of the criteria in Standards 6 and 7 effectively and in a well-managed and mature way, within a single piece of totally independent writing (one and a half sides or more)

- Write with at least 98% accuracy across all aspects of their writing, e.g.
  o text type/genre
  o response to stimulus or purpose
  o basic skills
  o 'writing voice'

A secure Standard 7 requires the production of a striking piece of writing, similar to that of a literate adult, although the stimulus may be more age appropriate. When asked, "How might this be appropriately improved?" there should be little or no improvement identifiable.

Children who are a 'Secure Standard 7' should easily meet the curriculumn expectations at the end of key stage 2.

STANDARD 7: Year 6/P7

Name: Date:

No	Criteria	Evidence? (✔, ✗, ●)
1	Can spell all vocabulary correctly apart from rare technical or obscure words. (Must have used unusual, ambitious vocabulary that is spelt correctly.)	
2	Can open and close writing in interesting, unusual or dramatic ways, when appropriate.	
3	Can use the full range of punctuation accurately and precisely, including for sub-division, effect, listing, direct speech, parenthesis, etc.	
4	Can write neatly, legibly, accurately and fluently, in a joined style.	
5	Can vary font for effect or emphasis when appropriate (print, italics or capitalization). There may only be one example.	
6	Can use a wide range of conventions appropriately to the context, e.g. paragraphs, sub and side headings, addendum, footnote, contents, etc.	
7	Can use a wide range of sophisticated connectives, including conjunctions, adverbs and prepositions, to show time, cause, sequence and mode, including to open sentences sometimes.	
8	Can use clauses confidently and appropriately for audience and purpose.	
9	Can use implicit links within a text, e.g. referring back to a point made earlier or forward to more information or detail to come.	
10	Can use complex groupings for effect, before or after the verb. (For example: 'How I love the warmth of the summer breeze, the lapping of the waves and the soft swishing of the sand beneath my sandals.') There may only be one example.	
11	Can use a range of techniques to interact or show awareness of the audience, e.g. action, dialogue, quotation, aside, suspense, tension, comment.	
12	Can write with maturity, confidence and imagination.	
13	Can adapt writing for the full range of purposes, always showing awareness of audience and purpose.	
14	Can consciously vary levels of formality according to purpose and audience.	
15	Can sustain a convincing viewpoint throughout the piece of writing, e.g. authoritative, expert, convincing portrayal of character, opposing opinions, etc.	
16	Can use a wide range of ambitious vocabulary accurately and precisely (they should be words that are not usually used by a child of that age).	
17	Can use two or more stylistic features to create effect within the text, e.g. rhetorical questions, repetition, figurative language, passive voice, metaphor, simile, alliteration, onomatopoeia, groupings, elaboration, nominalization, impersonal voice.	
18	Can use creative and varied sentence structures when appropriate, intermingling with simple structures for effect.	
19	Can always construct grammatically correct sentences, unless using dialect or alternative constructions consciously for effect.	
20	Can use pertinent and precise detail as appropriate.	
21	Can demonstrate a wide range of the criteria in Standard 7 effectively and in a well-managed and mature way, within a single piece of totally independent writing (of at least one and a half sides of A4).	

Assessment score

0–6 ticks = not yet working at this Standard; review against Standard 6.
7–10 ticks = Developing
11–17 ticks = Secure
18–21 ticks = Advanced

Exemplification of National Expectations

The following assessed samples of children's writing have been provided to show what 'Secure' at each Standard should look like. The assessor's notes against each criterion in the **Oxford Writing Criterion Scale** have also been provided for reference.

Pre-Writing Standard

Assessment score

Score = 15/15 (3 criteria not assessable so thresholds must be lowered by 3).

	Criteria	Evidence?	Notes
1	Will tolerate hand manipulation.	✔	Assume she is beyond this stage as she can write her own name.
2	Will work with another to allow mark-making using body parts or an implement.	✔	Assume she is beyond this stage as emergent words can be decoded.
3	Will attempt to mark-make independently.	✔	Emergent words show she is beyond this stage.
4	Can recognize mark-making materials.	✔	Assume she is beyond this stage as she can approximate words.
5	Can use and enjoys mark-making materials.	✔	Wrote willingly/cheerfully.
6	Can show some control in mark-making.	✔	Control shown through writing in three clear lines.
7	Can produce some recognizable letters.	✔	Almost every letter is identifiable.
8	Can differentiate between different letters and symbols.	–	Uncertain from this. Would need to provide a mix and ask her to pick out the letters.
9	Shows some awareness of sequencing of letters.	✔	The emergent words have key letters in the correct order and can be mainly decoded once we know what she says she has written.
10	Can copy over/under a model.	✔	The control of sequencing and of the letter shapes are beyond this stage.
11	Can imitate adults' writing and understands the purpose of writing.	✔	The emergent writing is beyond this stage.
12	Can name three or more different purposes of writing.	–	Would need to do a 'classroom walk' with her to assess this, 'spotting' writing and saying what job it does.
13	Can ascribe meaning to own mark-making, ('reads' what has been 'written').	✔	Rhia's response has been scribed below: 'A fairy cuddly toy / a cuddly toy / a doll'
14	Knows print has meaning and that, in English, it is read from left to right and top to bottom.	✔	There is a clear orientation in all three lines of emergent writing.
15	Can write the initial letter of their own name.	✔	The name at the bottom starts correctly with 'r'.
16	Can attempt to 'write' things, including their own name, using random letters.	✔	Has written her name at the bottom.
17	Can write their own name, although it may be with wrong letter formations or mixed lower/upper case.	✔	Has written her name at the bottom.
18	Can recognize their own first name, when it is written clearly in print.	–	Would need to do a 'classroom walk' with her to see if she can pick out her own peg, book, book bag or similar.

Standard 1: Reception/P1

Assessment score

0–2 ticks = not yet working at this Standard; review against Pre-Writing Standard.
3–8 ticks = Developing
9–16 ticks = Secure
17–19 ticks = Advanced
Assessment point: children with 18 or more ticks may be assessed against Standard 2.

Score = 6/14 (5 criteria not assessable so thresholds must be lowered by 5).
Judgement = Standard 1 Secure.

Exemplification of National Expectations

	Criteria	Evidence?	Notes
1	Can draw recognizable letters of the alphabet.	✔	Every letter is recognizable although size and shape are still erratic.
2	Can write their own name.	✔	Can write her own name with mainly appropriate upper/lower case letters, although size and shape are not fully controlled.
3	Can 'write' things using a mix of appropriate and random letters.	–	Not assessable.
4	Can sequence most of the letters of the alphabet.	–	Not assessable.
5	Can write their own name with correct letter formation, although size and shape may still be slightly inconsistent.	✔	Only the sizing is incorrect.
6	Can name the purpose of different texts/types of writing (at least three).	–	Not assessable.
7	Can 'read' what he/she has 'written'.	✔	Can assume so by this stage, but should confirm by asking her to 'read' her writing.
8	Can hold and use a pencil effectively.	✔	Is able to control the pencil well enough to shape most letters correctly.
9	Can spell some of the words from the Year R High Frequency Word list.	●	Only three words plus her name are correct, so not secure.
10	Can spell CVC (consonant, vowel, consonant) words (e.g. sit, bag, cat) usually correctly.	●	Not enough evidence.
11	Can write simple labels and captions.	✔	Neve's writing is beyond this stage.
12	Can usually leave a space between emerging words.	●	Not enough evidence as the size of her writing means there is usually only one word per line.
13	Can show some control over word order producing short logical statements, trying to use emergent phonics for spellings not known.	●	Only one statement given so not enough evidence to be secure.
14	Can produce two or more logical statements on the same subject.	✘	No evidence here.
15	Can spell many words on the Year R High Frequency Word List.	✘	This writing suggests spelling is weak. Should be assessed separately.
16	Is beginning to attempt to write simple known stories.	–	Would need to ask her to write other types of text over time, having taught them first.
17	Can say what they want to write, speaking in clearly defined statements or sentences.	–	Not assessable.
18	Can spell many common, single syllable words correctly in writing, including most of the words in the Year R High Frequency list and the Early Years Outcomes.	✘	See above comment on spelling.
19	Can write three or more simple statements on a given subject that can be read without the child's help and that make sense, although letter shapes and spelling may not be fully accurate.	✘	No evidence here.

Standard 2: Year 1/P2

Anna

I haD fun pooshlh
ELLa and I poosh
AryA it wos fuh
Bcos I wos poosh ih.
I slid Dah the sLiD
the wos frst.

Assessment score

0–6 ticks = not yet working at this Standard; review against Standard 1.
7–12 ticks = Developing
13–17 ticks = Secure
18–22 ticks = Advanced
Assessment point: children with 20 or more ticks may be assessed against Standard 3.

Score = 15/22.
Judgement = Standard 2 Secure.

	Criteria	Evidence?	Notes
1	Can write their own first name with appropriate upper and lower case letters (may not be totally accurate).	✔	'Anna'
2	Can form all letters clearly, although size and shape may be irregular.	✔	All letters are the correct shape, although size, upper/lower case and ascender/descenders are still erratic.
3	Writes simple regular words, some spelt correctly.	✔	10 words and name are spelt correctly and all words are decodable.
4	Almost always leaves spaces between words.	✔	Words have clear spaces before and after except at the end of lines.
5	Makes sensible phonic attempts at words.	✔	All words are decodable and logical in terms of phonics, except one: 'dan' for 'down', but it may be the way she speaks.
6	Can spell all CVC (consonant, vowel, consonant) words (e.g. sit, bag, cat) correctly.	●	Yes, but the piece is a little short for a secure judgement.
7	Confidently writes some captions and labels and attempts other simple forms of writing (e.g. lists, stories, retelling etc.).	✔	Writing is beyond this stage.
8	Can show some control over letter size, shape and orientation in writing.	●	Letter size, upper/lower case, ascender/descenders all need work.
9	Can say what their writing says and means.	✔	Writing is beyond this stage.
10	Can retell known stories in writing	✔	Writing is beyond this stage. This is a simple report (news) so she should be able to write a retelling.
11	Can produce their own ideas for writing (not a retelling).	✔	This is a simple report and her own news, so self-initiated.
12	Can show some control over word order, producing logical statements	✔	The flow of the piece is logical.
13	Can spell most of the Year R and 1 High Frequency words and the Year 1 words in the National Curriculum. Appendix 1.	●	A little short for a secure judgement.
14	Can make recognizable attempts at spelling words not known (almost all decodable without the child's help).	✔	All are decodable.
15	Can write simple texts such as lists, stories, reports, recounts (of a paragraph or more).	●	Borderline in length – would need more evidence for a secure judgement.
16	Begins to show awareness of how full stops are used in writing. (May be in the wrong places or only one, final full stop.)	✔	Emergent full stops are incorrect.
17	Can usually give letters a clear and regular size, shape and orientation (ascenders and descenders and use of upper and lower case are usually accurate).	✘	Not accurate.
18	Can use ANY connective (may only ever be 'and') to join two simple sentences, thoughts, ideas, etc.	✔	'and' and 'because' (spelt: 'Bcos').
19	Can use appropriate vocabulary (should be coherent and sensible) in more than three statements.	✔	Coherent and sensible.
20	Can always use logical phonic strategies when trying to spell unknown words in more than three statements.	✔	All except one ('dan') are logical.
21	Can usually use a capital letter and full stop, question mark or exclamation mark to punctuate sentences.	✘	Insecure on full stops and no other punctuation is used.
22	Can produce a paragraph or more of developed ideas independently that can be read without help from the child (must not be a retelling).	●	Needs a little more length. The size of the writing makes it look longer than it is.

Standard 3: Year 2/P3

Dear Mr Russell,

I am witing to you so you can take your class to The Living Rainforest. Me George Max in class 3 was tried wen we went there but I was exsitid wen we got there. Wen we get in we saw a carpit python it lookt ferogious, however the 3 toed sloth was quite the opposite, in addition to he was harmless at all, lots of the animals were lovly

What we did we had amazing. Trip as well as that it was hot and sticy. We saw a dumb plan to If you eat it you wont be abell to tork because your mouth will swel up. We saw a maxical plarnt. Sumone pord water on it and sumhow bounced of. you will have a lovly time.

Thank you For reeding my leter
        yous sincereey
            George
            Max

	Criteria	Evidence?	Notes
1	Can communicate ideas and meaning confidently in a series of sentences of at least a paragraph in length. (May not be accurate, but mainly 'flows'.)	✔	Yes. Length and 'flow' are both good.
2	Can control use of ascenders/descenders and upper/lower case letters in handwriting.	●	Writing is becoming regular in size, but not controlled. Use of capitals and ascenders / descenders are not always secure.
3	Can write in three or more text forms with reasonable accuracy.	✔	This is a letter, so it can be assumed that all three early text forms are also secure.
4	Can provide enough detail to interest the reader.	✔	The descriptions are often interesting and sometimes the voice is strong.
5	Can vary the structure of sentences to interest the reader (e.g. questions, direct speech or opening with a subordinate clause, etc.).	✔	There are two strong openings ('When…' and 'If…'). There is also use of sophisticated connectives to extend sentences/add a clause ('however', 'in addition').
6	Can sometimes use interesting and ambitious words (they should be words not usually used by a child of that age, and not a technical word used in a taught context only).	✔	'ferocious', 'opposite', 'harmless', 'magical'.
7	Can usually sustain narrative and non-narrative forms (can write at length – close to a side of A4 at least – staying on task).	●	A little short; one more good paragraph would have made a secure judgement possible.
8	Can match organization to purpose.	✔	The letter structure is secure (NB: the address has been removed for publication).
9	Can usually maintain the use of basic sentence punctuation (full stops followed by capital letters) in a piece close to a side of A4 in length.	●	Writing is often missing capital letters after the full stops. One sentence in the first paragraph is too long.
10	Can spell most common words correctly and most of the Years R, 1 & 2 High Frequency Words, and the Year 1 & 2 words in the National Curriculum. Appendix 1.	●	Easier words like 'tired', 'when', 'sticky' 'swell', 'talk' and 'off' are incorrect.
11	Can use phonetically plausible strategies to spell or attempt to spell unknown polysyllabic words.	✔	All spellings are logical and decodable, except 'plarnt' which is not logical for 'plant' unless the speaker speaks with received pronunciation.
12	Can use connectives other than 'and' to join two or more simple sentences, thoughts, ideas, etc. (e.g. but, so, then, or, when, if, that, because).	✔	'so', 'when', 'but', 'however', 'in addition', 'as well as' etc.
13	Can use a range of punctuation, mainly correctly, including at least three of the following: full stop and capital letter, exclamation mark, question mark, comma (at least in lists), apostrophe for simple contraction and for singular possession (at least).	✘	Punctuation is weak; full stops and capitals are not maintained throughout and there are only four commas.
14	Can make their writing lively and interesting (e.g. provides additional detail, consciously uses humour, varies sentence length or uses punctuation to create effect, etc.).	✔	Poor punctuation makes this judgement hard, but if it is read out correctly it has strengths, mainly because of the connectives and the additional details.
15	Can link ideas and events, using strategies to create 'flow'.	✔	Through connectives, e.g. 'When we went…', 'When we got in…', '…in addition…', 'If you eat it you…'
16	Can use adjectives and descriptive phrases for detail and emphasis (consciously selects the adjective for purpose).	✔	E.g. 'ferocious', 'harmless', 'lovely', 'amazing', 'hot and sticky', 'magical'.
17	Structures basic sentences correctly, including capitals and full stops in a longer piece (one error is acceptable).	●	Sentence structure is a weakness in this piece.
18	Can use accurate and consistent handwriting (can show consistent use of upper/lower case, ascenders/descenders, size and form).	✘	Writing is becoming controlled, but use of capitals and ascenders/descenders are not always secure and size and shape are still irregular.
19	Begins to show evidence of joined handwriting.	✔	There is secure evidence of joining, but only a little.
20	Uses past and present tenses correctly.	●	There are grammar weaknesses, but only one tense error: 'get'.
21	Can produce close to a side (or more) of A4 writing that is clear and coherent with one or more strong features.	●	The writing is a little too short. No strong features other than the striking use of connectives.

Standard 4: Year 3/P4

Dear Ashad,

I'm writing to you because I would love for your class, three to go to The living Rainforest because st___ class three traveled to the living Rainforest and had a AMAZING!! time, you would love it yourself.

When we got there and a lady got a Rule sheet to give to the grownups:
1) Don't shout
2) Don't touch Anything
3) Don't feed the Animals
Then we had askart to go to a gift shop. After we had a Play in the playground When time went by we had a tour and Saw lots of exciting animals including a daager crocodile who was sleeping lucy, Guppies, a rippiling sting Ray. When we fineshed our tour we had a yummy lunch.

In Addution to that we got a Play in the Play Ground. Afterwards we got to go back into the greenhouse, to draw pitires to the Animals. The guppies were easy because they were Just like cold fish. We had to go home It dintit take that long to get back or there.

your Sincerly
Hasif

Exemplification of National Expectations

	Criteria	Evidence?	Notes
1	Can produce work which is organized, imaginative and clear (e.g. simple opening and ending).	✔	Writing uses a letter structure and paragraphs for organization.
2	Can usually join their handwriting.	✔	Writing is mainly joined.
3	Can use a range of chosen forms appropriately and consistently.	✔	This is a letter, so it can be assumed that all three early text forms are also secure.
4	Can adapt their chosen form to the audience (e.g. provide information about characters or setting, make a series of points, use brackets, etc.).	✔	Letter structure / paragraphs to organise / provides information / direct appeal to reader.
5	Can sometimes use interesting and ambitious words (they should be words not usually used by a child of that age, and not a technical word used in a taught context only).	●	The writing contains good vocabulary ('amazing', 'including', 'In addition . . .'), but not truly ambitious words.
6	Can develop and extend ideas logically in sequenced sentences (but they may still be overly detailed or brief).	✔	Secure.
7	Can extend sentences using a wider range of connectives to clarify relationships between points and ideas (e.g. when, because, if, after, while, also, as well).	✔	Uses simple connectives plus: 'because', 'When', 'After. . .', 'including'.
8	Can usually use correct grammatical structures in sentences (nouns and verbs generally agree).	●	There are some grammatical errors, e.g. the word 'had' is added in 'we had askad to . . .' etc.
9	Can use pronouns appropriately to avoid the awkward repetition of nouns.	✔	Secure, e.g. 'I', 'you', 'we', 'they'.
10	Can use most punctuation accurately, including at least three of the following: full stop and capital letter, question mark, exclamation mark, comma, apostrophe.	✔	The writing contains full stops, commas, exclamation marks (slightly misused), and apostrophes.
11	Can structure and organize work clearly (e.g. beginning, middle, end; letter structure; dialogue structure).	✔	Yes. This is a letter with paragraphs and an embedded list.
12	Is beginning to use paragraphs.	✔	This is secure.
13	Can adapt form and style for purpose (e.g. there is a clear difference between formal and informal letters; use of abbreviated sentences in notes and diaries, etc.).	✔	This is the standard form for a factual report within a letter.
14	Can write neatly, legibly and accurately, mainly in a joined style.	●	Handwriting is mainly joined, but very irregular in size and often poorly formed. There are capitals in the wrong places.
15	Can use adjectives and adverbs for description.	✔	E.g. 'amazing', 'exciting', 'rippling', 'yummy'.
16	Can spell phonetically regular, or familiar common polysyllabic words accurately and most or all of the Year 3 High Frequency Words and the Year 3 words in the National Curriculum Appendix 1.	●	Most regular words are correct. There are some errors (e.g. 'traveled', 'askad', 'dwafen', 'rippiling').
17	Can develop characters and describe settings, feelings and/or emotions, etc.	●	The features in this piece are not developed enough to give a secure judgement.
18	Can link and relate events, including past, present and future, sensibly (afterwards, before, also, after a while, eventually, etc.).	✔	Linking is secure, e.g. 'When . . .', 'Then . . .', 'After . . .', 'In addition . . .', 'Afterwards . . .'.
19	Can attempt to give opinion, interest or humour through detail.	✔	He gives an opinion on the visit and on what he has seen.
20	Can use generalizing words for style (e.g. sometimes, never, always, often, mainly, mostly, generally, etc.) and/or modal verbs/the conditional tense (e.g. might do it, may go, could rain, should win).	●	E.g. 'lots of', but not enough to be judged as secure.
21	Is beginning to develop a sense of pace (writing is lively and interesting).	✔	The writing is quite lively.

Oxford Primary Writing Assessment

Standard 5: Year 4/P5

12 Long Croft
Barrow
1st April

Dear David Webb,

I am writing this to say a BIG thankyou for coming in to our school and doing the workshop.

To begin with, I thought the workshop was amazing and spectacular! Also I have learnt loads about books. I really enjoyd planning our own story.

Our class is reading one of your books and it's magnificent, the book called Eye of the storm. Your books are so good maybe I would like to be a writer too "How do you make your books so cool."

When we were in the hall I was so scared to come up and look in your bag because I didn't want to and I didn't know what was in the bag?

I want to say a BIG thankyou for coming in our school and teaching us different things about books. I really enjoyd it and I hope you did too. Your different subjects did teach us lots!

"What will your next book be called?" If you know what it will be called anyway.

Thankyou for coming!
Your sincerly,
Bethan.

Assessment score

0–5 ticks = not yet working at this Standard; review against Standard 4.
6–9 ticks = Developing
10–15 ticks = Secure
16–19 ticks = Advanced
Assessment point: children with 17 or more ticks may be assessed against Standard 6.

Score = 12/19.
Judgement = Standard 5 Secure.

Exemplification of National Expectations

	Criteria	Evidence?	Notes
1	Can write in a lively and coherent style.	✔	Writing is lively and clear.
2	Can use a range of styles and genres confidently and independently. (If the writing is a narrative, simple report or recount of a known story this cannot be ticked as they should already know these forms.)	✔	Letter structure and paragraphing are correct, so it can be assumed that all three early text forms are secure.
3	Can sometimes use interesting and ambitious words (they should be words not usually used by a child of that age, and not a technical word used in a taught context only).	●	E.g. 'spectacular', 'magnificent',
4	Can organize ideas appropriately for both purpose and reader (e.g. captions, headings, bullets, fonts, chapters, letter formats, paragraphs, logically sequenced events, contextual and background information etc.).	✔	The letter structure is secure (NB: the address has been removed for publication) and there is contextual background in the opening paragraph.
5	Can use a wide range of punctuation mainly accurately, including at least three of the following: full stop and capital letter, question mark, exclamation mark, apostrophe and comma.	✔	The writing contains commas, full stops, an exclamation mark, speech marks (although not quite in the right context), an apostrophe, question mark (used once and missed once).
6	Can write neatly, legibly and accurately, usually maintaining a joined style.	✔	Handwriting is joined and mainly neat.
7	Can use more sophisticated connectives (e.g. although, however, nevertheless, despite, contrary to, as well as, etc.).	✗	There are no connectives beyond 'when', 'also', 'because'.
8	Can use links to show time and cause.	✔	E.g. 'To begin with…', 'also…', 'maybe…', 'when', 'because'
9	Can open sentences in a wide range of ways for interest and impact.	✔	'To begin with…', 'Your books are so good…', 'When…'
10	Can use paragraphs, although they may not always be accurate.	✔	Paragraphs are a little short sometimes.
11	Can produce thoughtful and considered writing (uses simple explanation, opinion, justification and deduction).	✔	There is an explanation of the context in the opening and opinion (e.g. 'I thought the workshop was amazing…', 'Your books are so good…', '…I was so scared to…' etc). There is also justification (e.g. '…because I didn't want to and I didn't know what was in the bag.').
12	Can use or attempt grammatically complex structures (e.g. expansion before and after the noun: 'The little, old man who lived on the hill…', '…by the lady who taught me the guitar…'; subordinate clauses: 'I felt better when…', etc.).	●	Opens one sentence with a clause, but mainly uses standard structures.
13	Can spell unfamiliar regular polysyllabic words accurately and most or all of the Year 4 High Frequency Words and the Year 4 words in the National Curriculum Appendix 1.	✔	Spelling is good – there is only one error. 'Enjoyed' is used twice.
14	Can use nouns, pronouns and tenses accurately and consistently throughout.	●	There are some small grammatical errors and slightly incorrect language structures (e.g. '…I was so scared to come…', 'Was there different objects…', etc.
15	Can use apostrophes and/or inverted commas, mainly accurately. (If direct speech is not appropriate to the task, apostrophes alone can score the tick).	●	Apostrophes are used correctly twice in the same word, but speech marks are not quite used correctly.
16	Can select from a range of known adventurous vocabulary for a purpose, with some words being particularly well chosen.	✗	There is no evidence in this piece.
17	Can select interesting strategies to move a piece of writing forward (e.g. asides, characterization, dialogue with the audience, dialogue etc.).	✔	Maintains a good dialogue with the reader (an author).
18	Can advise assertively, although not confrontationally, in factual writing (e.g. 'An important thing to think about before deciding…', 'We always need to think about…', etc.).	✔	E.g. 'Your books are so good, maybe I would…' 'I want to say…', 'I really enjoyed it and…'
19	Can develop ideas in creative and interesting ways.	●	The emergent skills demonstrated in the writing will soon become strengths with good teaching.

Standard 6: Year 5/P6

Tuesday 3rd December

Sir John Barrow Primary School
Argyle Street
Ulverston
Cymbria
Dear Sir/Madam,   LA12 0BD

I am a Yr5 pupil called Islay Reddy at the wonderful SJB (well not so wonderful) you, the Goveners, are taking away the playtimes of children such as myself. I abore the repugnant idea of not having playtimes, how would you feel if we took something precious off you?
My first point is; children from every age need fresh-air otherwise they'll grow to be very unhealthy, fat children. Eventhough maths and litracy are important, children still need a run around. It is ovious children need fresh-air, they need to fell the summer breeze slowly fly majesticly past their face or run around with their tummies full of gorgeous warm food whilst throwing snowballs at each other Can't you see, they need to frolick in the wind, rain, sun, snow.
Evedince suggests that the behavour improves if they have playtimes because they need to run out some steam and talk to each other as they're not allow to talk in class because they need to learn. Have you had any other complaint?

Only a fool would think that not allowing children to have playtimes is a ridiculous idea and if you bans that you will also be banning lunchtime clubs such as:
Miss Porters club
Chess club
Debate club
and many more so please don't ban playtimes because it can also effect forest schools. Forest schools is important for children to get outdoors and have fun. Just like playtimes !!!
I'm sure you will agree that buying lots of wonderful equitment like the shining metal chain bridge, the new fence around the football pitch and the coal black tyre park.

My final point is that children need exersise eventhough they go to school maybe on a bike or scooter and back whereas they still need more just like a five a day. I hear that Mrs Herganain who is the chair of Goveners, ha children at this school so tell her to ask her children what they think.

I hope you will take in my points like;
• Exersise
• Behavour
• Forest schools
• Money
• Talking
Thank you for taking youre time to read this letter I am looking forward to your response.
                    Yours Sincerely
                    Islay Josephine
                    Reddy

	Criteria	Evidence?	Notes
1	Can produce well-structured and organized writing using a range of conventions in layout.	✔	Accurate letter structure with embedded lists (hybrid text).
2	Can use appropriate informal and formal styles with confidence.	✔	Strong, persuasive voice with a good level of indignation and occasional incredulity.
3	Can select the correct genre for audience and purpose, and use it accurately.	✔	Good use of a hybrid text, with lists within a letter.
4	Can select from a wide range of known imaginative and ambitious vocabulary (they should be words that are not usually used by a child of that age) and use them precisely.	●	Demonstrates quite a good range of ambitious vocabulary, e.g. 'abhor', 'repugnant', 'majestically', 'whilst', 'frolic', 'improves', 'effect' but not all are spelt correctly.
5	Can use paragraphs consistently and appropriately.	✔	Paragraphing is used accurately.
6	Can group things appropriately before or after a main verb (e.g. 'The books, the pens and the pencils were all ready on the table').	✔	Contains a very good complex grouping: '... wonderful equipment like the shining metal chain bridge, the new fence around the football pitch and the coal black tyre park.'
7	Can use all grammar accurately except when consciously using dialect or colloquialism for purpose and audience.	✔	There is one grammatical error: 'Forest Schools is important', however this is often used as a label, which might explain the error. '...run out more steam...' is a local colloquialism.
8	Can use different techniques to open or conclude work appropriately.	✘	There is no evidence in this piece.
9	Can use complex sentence structures appropriately.	✔	There are many good examples.
10	Can use a wider range of punctuation, almost always accurately, to include three or more of the following: comma, apostrophe, bullets, inverted commas, hyphen, brackets, colon or semi-colon.	✔	The writing includes the use of commas, brackets, full stops, question marks, semi-colons (although one is not used correctly), apostrophes, colons, exclamation marks and bullets.
11	Can use punctuation appropriately to create effect.	●	Question marks and brackets. No ellipsis or dashes.
12	Can write neatly, legibly and accurately in a flowing, joined style.	✔	Handwriting is neat, joined and easily read.
13	Can adapt handwriting for a range of tasks and purposes.	✘	No opportunities have been created for this.
14	Can spell accurately in all but the most complex words and most or all of the Year 5 High Frequency Words and the Year 5 words in the National Curriculum Appendix 1.	●	There are some weaknesses, e.g. 'Goveners', 'abore', 'ovious', 'majesticly', 'frolick', 'evedince', 'behavouir'.
15	Can use the passive voice for variety and to shift focus.	✘	There is no evidence in the piece.
16	Can use a range of narrative techniques with confidence, interweaving elements when appropriate (e.g. action, dialogue, quotation, formal or informal style, aside, observation, suspense).	✔	The writing demonstrates a formal style, with an aside in brackets and questions.
17	Can vary sentence length and word order confidently to sustain interest.	✔	E.g. 'Just like playtimes!'
18	Can use a range of devices to adapt writing to the needs of the reader.	✔	The introductory paragraph sets the context; lists, parenthesis and a summary in bullets are included.
19	Can use literary features to create effect.	●	The writing demonstrates good attempts at imagery and metaphor but they are not quite managed correctly, e.g. '...feel the summer breeze slowly fly majestically past their face...', '...to run out (off) more steam...'
20	Can interweave implicit and explicit links between sections.	✔	'My first point is...', 'Even though...', 'My final point...' are all explicit links. The writing constantly refers back to the subject through phrases like 'It is obvious that...', 'Can't you see...', 'Evidence suggests...' etc. (implicit links).
21	Can use punctuation to show division between clauses, to indicate, to vary pace, to create atmosphere or to sub-divide.	●	Some punctuation within sentences is missing or inaccurate and the list of three examples of clubs would be better as a grouping.
22	Can show confident and established 'voice'.	●	A well-managed and interesting piece, but there are many areas for development.

Standard 7: Year 6/P7

Cell 13,
Deepest Dungeon,
His Majesty's Prison
Waterside Rd
9th May 1910

Dearest Ratty,

No doubt word has reached you ~~to~~ of my current-and dismal-whereabouts. Indeed, the romours are true! You, Badger and Mole always knew best: I know you will never forgive me, but I deeply hope that you will try to understand why I did what I did.

Obviously, you will already know the beginning of my story (when you tried to help me, but, ~~asthe~~ the stubborn toad that I am, ~~resoloute~~ declined all help) but for the rest of the events you will have pieced together an inaccurate and untruthful version; probably not one that threw me into the best light!

To help you understand, I have enclosed an extract from yesterday's newspaper. Hopefully, it will be informative...

THE RIVERSIDE TIMES
Volume 12
Issue 7

The Toad that Fought the Law...

The Crown Court recently had an unusual defendent on stand. Mr. Toad (aged 26) has a reputation among his fellow animals for being stubborn, a spoilt but kind-hearted creature who squanders his inheritance of over £200,000! Earlier today Mr. Toad surprised us all.

Being so wealthy, most would assume that he would have no need for thieving: Toad, however, proved them wrong. Toady inexplicably felt the need to take a motor car that was left unattended outside the Red Lion Pub.

With these clear allegations against him, the pompous P.T.O

amphibean had no chance when his case was taken to court. Consequently, the toad was sentenced to 20 long years in His Majesty's Prison. He was dragged away screaming... "I am innocent!"

Reported by Niamh Berry

The cheek of it! 'The pompous amphibian', 'spoilt, stubborn'! I don't know what an 'amphibian' is, but it doesn't sound particularly friendly! Frankly, I suppose I am 'spoilt' and 'stubborn' but there is such a thing as tact.

I will surely perish in here, while this dark cloud of death hangs over me. Never have I realised how much I relished life on the riverbank. I miss the lush green fields, I miss the happy gurgle of the river, I miss the trips to your boat, I miss YOU, Mole and Badger, but most of all I miss the open road. I can feel the humming engines echoing past me in the world from above. Poop, poop...

Spare me a kind thought now and then, Ratty. And know that I will always be thinking of you as I deteriorate in this detestable, dank hole.

Give my love to Mole, Badger and all who reside on the river bank.

Yours Sincerely,
F~~~~~
(Toad of Toad Hall)

	Criteria	Evidence?	Notes
1	Can spell all vocabulary correctly apart from rare technical or obscure words.	✔	There are no errors.
2	Can open and close writing in interesting, unusual or dramatic ways, when appropriate.	●	The opening is interesting although not 'gripping' but the ending is standard.
3	Can use the full range of punctuation accurately and precisely, including for sub-division, effect, listing, direct speech, parenthesis, etc.	✔	Punctuation used: commas, parenthesis through dashes, brackets, exclamation marks, colons, apostrophe, ellipsis, speech marks, quotation marks. There is one questionable use of a colon.
4	Can write neatly, legibly, accurately and fluently, in a joined style.	●	Handwriting is very good, confident and clear but not joined.
5	Can vary font for effect or emphasis when appropriate (print, italics or capitalization).	✔	The writer uses capitalization in the newspaper article heading and italics for the sub-heading and for emphasis.
6	Can use a wide range of conventions appropriately to the context, e.g. paragraphs, sub and side headings, addendum, footnote, contents, etc.	✔	The writing uses paragraphs, heading and sub-headings, letter features and journalistic features.
7	Can use a wide range of sophisticated connectives, including conjunctions, adverbs and prepositions, to show time, cause, sequence and mode, including to open sentences sometimes.	●	The writing uses most of the standard connectives, plus: 'being' and 'consequently'. More opportunities should have been created.
8	Can use clauses confidently and appropriately for audience and purpose.	✔	This is very well maintained throughout.
9	Can use implicit links within a text, e.g. referring back to a point made earlier or forward to more information or detail to come.	✔	Refers back to prior events (e.g. 'Obviously you will already know the beginnings of my story…') and makes predictions (e.g. 'Hopefully it will be…').
10	Can use complex groupings for effect, before or after the verb.	✔	There is a wonderful example of a complex grouping, opening with: 'Never have I realised…'.
11	Can use a range of techniques to interact or show awareness of the audience, e.g. action, dialogue, quotation, aside, suspense, tension, comment.	✔	The clever use of a hybrid text provides increased opportunity for a range of techniques: quotation in the report, protest, indignation, quotation of parts of the report by Toad, nostalgia in the grouping, appeal towards the end.
12	Can write with maturity, confidence and imagination.	✔	The only improvement would be to create opportunity for a wider range of sophisticated connectives.
13	Can adapt writing for the full range of purposes, always showing awareness of audience and purpose.	✔	Maintains the consistent, slightly 'pompous' voice of Toad throughout the letter, whilst intermingling indignation, deference and direct appeal.
14	Can consciously vary levels of formality according to purpose and audience.	✔	The pompous, 'flowery' language of Toad (maintained throughout letter) contrasts with the impersonal voice of the newspaper report – formal, factual and slightly inflammatory.
15	Can sustain a convincing viewpoint throughout the piece of writing.	✔	The writer consciously changes Toad's viewpoint – moving between indignation, denial, nostalgia and desperation.
16	Can use a wide range of ambitious vocabulary accurately and precisely (they should be words that are not usually used by a child of that age).	✔	There are no breath-taking words, but the vocabulary is extremely good, spelt correctly and used precisely. E.g. 'dismal', 'squanders', 'inheritance', 'allegations', 'pompous'.
17	Can use two or more stylistic features to create effect within the text.	✔	Stylistic features used: metaphor, personification, onomatopoeia, alliteration.
18	Can use creative and varied sentence structures when appropriate, intermingling with simple structures for effect.	✔	Most sentences in the body of the letter are varied and creative. Good examples of the short sentence or phrase for impact: "I am innocent!", 'The cheek of it!', 'Poop, poop…'
19	Can always construct grammatically correct sentences, unless using dialect or alternative constructions consciously for effect.	✔	There are no grammatical errors.
20	Can use pertinent and precise detail as appropriate.	✔	E.g. acknowledgement of prior failings in the second paragraph and things he will miss in the complex grouping.
21	Can demonstrate a wide range of the criteria in Standard 7 effectively and in a well-managed and mature way, within a single piece of totally independent writing.	●	17 out of 21.

Setting Targets to Ensure Progress

Target setting, combined with Assessment for Learning, is a crucial element in enabling children to make progress in their writing and achieve their maximum potential.

Effective target setting relies on the professional judgement of the teacher and should be based on a detailed scrutiny of each child's current performance as well as knowledge of how they learn. However, a framework for setting short and medium term targets is provided here as a guide for teachers to use and adapt as necessary.

Medium Term Targets

Medium term targets are informed by the latest summative assessment conducted using the OWCS and should be achievable by the start of the next term. It is not feasible to give a precise formula for identifying medium term targets, as they are reactive to the evidence in the piece assessed. However, they should generally be directed at one or more of the following:

● Criteria that show (by a dot) that the child is beginning to show evidence of using the skill, but is not yet secure.

● Criteria that show (by a dot) that the child is using the skill, but not yet accurately enough.

● Criteria that will move a child who is currently 'on track' further forward at a more accelerated pace.

● Criteria that show (by a cross) that a child is not yet using a skill but you know he/she should be at this stage.

● General basic skills such as consistent spelling, punctuation and/or handwriting.

Dotted criteria are usually the easiest to secure in the medium term because with good teaching and coaching the child should secure these skills within the term and be able to move forward.

That said, if you know that the child could have demonstrated the skill securely – they just did not for the assessed piece of writing – you should have an Assessment for Learning (AfL) conversation with the child, showing where the piece falls short of secure assessment and stressing the importance of 'showing off' his or her best skills. The child may have this skill as a 'quick win' short term target (see opposite), but should not need it as a medium term target.

Medium term targets should focus on basic skills – spelling, punctuation and/or handwriting – as a priority if these remain a weakness but for the most part should focus on the following skills as a means to accelerate progress:

● Using a wider range of ambitious vocabulary (WOW words)

● Using a wider range of sentence openings including Power Openers (connectives, 'ly' and 'ing' words)

● Using a wider range of punctuation, including Power Punctuation (! ? …) for effect.

● Using a wider range of connectives/more sophisticated connectives (conjunctions, adverbs, prepositions) to link ideas (e.g. although, despite, in spite of, as well as, contrary to, etc.).

● Using paragraphs accurately.

● Using literary features (see OWCS Standards 6 and 7).

For each of these medium term targets, the skill must be broken down into small steps to enable the learner to 'climb' successfully towards achievement. (See opposite.)

What about criteria marked with a X?

Criteria marked with a cross on the summative assessment will indicate one of the following:

- The child has not yet been taught this skill or aspect of writing.

- The child has been taught this skill fairly recently but is not demonstrating independent use just yet.

- The child has been taught this skill – and has many opportunities to practise and apply it – but is still not demonstrating it in independent writing.

If the first two judgements are the case, then these skills simply need to inform a teacher's medium to long term planning for the year (as appropriate). If the third judgement is the case then this skill MUST be included as a priority medium term target for that child – with some one-to-one support to help them if appropriate.

Short Term Targets

Short term targets in the form of 'small step targets' are essential to success in learning key skills, for many children. They reduce learning into bite-sized chunks that a child can understand clearly, learn easily and then demonstrate confidently.

Small step targets should be achievable within one day, one week or – at most – two weeks. They should be used to inform weekly observation and marking of children's writing and adjusted or changed as and when appropriate.
There are usually two types of small step targets:

1. 'Quick wins' that address skills that you know are already within the capability of the child, but that they have not demonstrated in their assessed writing.

2. Small step targets that are part of a progressive ladder towards achieving a medium term target.

1. Quick Wins

Immediate targets or 'quick wins' are identified either through the termly summative assessment using the OWCS or through marking the writing children do each week. They should only be set for those skills that the writer is very close to securing. It is possible that a child might not be set a quick win' target if the skills they need to focus on require a number of steps to achieve. By giving a 'quick win' target in marking, the teacher is reinforcing the message that they know the child can do this and that they need to show it every time they write.

As soon as the child is securely and consistently demonstrating the skill, the 'quick win' target should be changed. The teacher will need, however, to continue to monitor for its use and should maintain it as a focus for AfL conversations.

There are many possibilities for 'quick win' targets, but examples include:

- Always write neatly and clearly (for a child who sometimes does)

- Always use a capital letter after a full stop (for a child who sometimes does)

- Use a wider range of punctuation, including exclamation mark, question mark and ellipsis, for effect (for a child who understands how to use all of these, but doesn't)

- Use a wider range of ambitious words (for a child who has a good range of vocabulary, but only uses one or two ambitious words in a longer piece).

2. Progressive small step targets

Once the medium term targets have been identified following the summative assessment process (see page 50) a pathway towards achieving these targets needs to be put in place in order to raise the child's achievement in that aspect of their writing. Medium term targets will often take some weeks or longer to achieve so the teacher needs to break the skill down into a series of small steps that will enable the child to move forward confidently and successfully until the whole skill has been mastered.

Examples of skills that might require small step targets towards medium term targets are:

- Handwriting that is below the expectation for a child of that age
- Spelling that is below the expectation for a child of that age
- Punctuation use that is below the expectation for a child of that age
- Grammar that is inaccurate
- Length of writing that is below the expectation for a child of that age
- Detail and description that is below the expectation for a child of that age
- In schools that do *Big Writing*, use of one or more of the VCOP features that is below the expectation for a child of that age.

In Reception/P1, the small steps towards a medium term target are primarily for the benefit of the teacher – and parent, if appropriate – to enable them to plan the immediate next steps necessary for each child. They do not need to be shared directly with the child, although small aspects may be given orally to gently encourage progress.

From Year 1/P2 onwards the small steps towards each medium term target can be presented as **Child Speak Targets** and given directly to children so that they can use them meaningfully in the AfL process. A skills progression for each aspect of writing – with accompanying Child Speak Targets – is provided on pages 56–69.

How to set progressive small step targets

Following a summative assessment of a child's writing, using the OWCS, follow the steps below to identify appropriate small step targets towards each medium term target.

Step	What to do	Notes
1	Look at the dots on the child's summative assessment using the OWCS. Should any of these be 'quick wins'?	Set quick win targets as appropriate.
2	Look at the remaining dots and any crosses that identify skills that really *should* be secure, as well as the child's overall basic skills: spelling, punctuation, handwriting.	These inform your medium term targets.
3	For each medium term target, identify the skill or aspect of writing that the weakness relates to.	Refer to the relevant Progressive Skills Ladders and Child Speak Targets on pages 56–69
4	Photocopy the Progressive Skills Ladder/s for that child – adding their name and the date at the top.	
5	Work through the targets from the beginning, ticking any that the child has already shown they can do consistently.	You do not need to carry on beyond the Year or Key Stage that the child is working in.
6	Identify the small steps (Child Speak Targets) within the strand that the child cannot do.	i.e. those steps that are not ticked
7	Set up to three of these steps as the personal Target/s for the child, with any from earlier Year groups being the priority to secure.	If a pupil would benefit from it, the targets can be broken down into even smaller steps, for example: learning of one specific piece of punctuation.

Effective Target Setting: Exemplification

The following examples of short and medium term targets have been set based on the summative assessments of children's writing using the OWCS. The children's writing and associated assessments can be found on pages 34–49. The small step targets for each medium term target are sequential and should be given to the child one a a time to provide clear focus.

Rhia (Pre-Writing Standard)

Medium term targets	Small step targets
Work on letter size and shapes	• Can form every letter of the alphabet. • Can write some regular words, making the letters similar in size. • Can usually write all letters the same size.
Learn the High Frequency Words for Reception (in clusters)	• Can spell some words on the Reception High Frequency Word lists. • Is beginning to use some phonic skills to write some simple words.
Shared writing of the same two sentences each day until grasped	• 'Today is Monday. I am going to play.' (Change the two sentences once grasped.)

Neve (Standard 1: Reception)

Medium term targets	Small step targets
Learn the High Frequency Words for Reception (in clusters) and spell CVC words correctly	• Can spell some words on the Reception High Frequency Word lists. • Is beginning to use some phonic skills to write some simple words.
Work on letter size and shapes	• Can write some regular words, making the letters similar in size. • Is beginning to write both capital letters and lower case letters, saying which they are. • Can usually write all letters the same size.
Use talk to extend ideas towards writing three or more statements on a subject.	• Is learning a wide range of words. • Is speaking in full sentences. • Is beginning to join simple sentences to make longer ones. • Is beginning to add simple descriptions.

Anna (Standard 2: Year 1)

Medium term targets	Small step targets / Child speak targets
Basic skills are a priority. Work on letter size and shapes	• I always use capital and lower case letters correctly. • I can draw sticks above the other letters and tails below the line of writing. • I can always write on the line, with ascenders showing clearly above the small letters and descenders below the line.
Learn the spelling of High Frequency words for Reception and Year 1 and the Year 1 words in the N. C. Appendix 1	• I can spell half or more of the words on the Reception High Frequency Word lists. • I can spell all the words on the Reception High Frequency Word lists. • I can spell some words on the Year 1 High Frequency Word lists.
Punctuation – accurate use of full stops.	• I can put full stops into a short piece of writing that is understood. • I can use some full stops and capital letters to show most sentences in my writing. • I can usually use full stops and capital letters to show most sentences in my writing.

Max (Standard 3: Year 2)

Medium term targets	Small step targets / Child speak targets
Basic skills are a priority. Maintain neat, accurate handwriting	• I can always write on the line, with ascenders showing clearly above the small letters and descenders below the line. • I can maintain neat, well-formed writing for a paragraph or more. • I am starting to join all my writing.
Spelling of High Frequency words and Year 1 words in the N. C. Appendix 1	• I can spell all the words on the Year 1 National Curriculum word lists and the Year 1 High Frequency Word List correctly. • I can always spell common single syllable words correctly. • I can spell some of the words from the Year 2 National Curriculum word lists and the High Frequency Word List for Year 2 correctly.
Punctuation – especially to demarcate sentences.	• I always use full stops and capital letters accurately to show sentences in my writing. • I am beginning to use commas in my writing. • I can put commas in the correct places in sentences.

Hasif (Standard 4: Year 3)

Medium term targets	Small step targets / Child speak targets
Basic skills are a priority. Maintain neat, accurate handwriting	• I can maintain neat, well-formed writing for a paragraph or more. • I can maintain accurate formation of all letters. • I can maintain neat, regular writing for up to a side of A4 or more.
Spelling	• I can always spell common words correctly. • I can spell some of the words from the Year 3 National Curriculum word lists and the High Frequency Word List for Year 3 correctly. • I can spell all of the words from the Year 2 National Curriculum word lists and the High Frequency Word List for Year 2 correctly.
Use a wider range of truly ambitious vocabulary (WOW words) including adjectives and adverbs	• I can use a range of 'WOW' words (ambitious vocabulary) in my writing. • I can use a wide range of vocabulary that is ambitious for my age, correctly in my writing. • I can choose interesting vocabulary that is ambitious for my age, will engage the reader and is particularly appropriate for the writing task.

Bethan (Standard 5: Year 4)

Medium term targets	Small step targets / Child speak targets
n/a	'Quick win' small step target: • I can use inverted commas (speech marks) to show direct speech.
n/a	'Quick win' small step target: • I can use a wide range of vocabulary that is ambitious for my age, correctly in my writing.
Use a wider range of higher level connectives, including to open sentences.	• I can use more sophisticated connectives in my writing. *(E.g. although, however, nevertheless, as well as, despite, contrary to, in spite of, etc.)* • I can use more sophisticated links and sequence phrases in my writing. *(E.g. eventually, as a result of, in addition to, in spite of, as well as, a little while later, soon after that, since, etc.)* • I can use more sophisticated connectives to open sentences in my writing. *(E.g. Although…, However…, Despite…, Contrary to…)*

Islay (Standard 6: Year 5)

Medium term targets	Small step targets / Child speak targets
Accurate use of all spelling, except the most unusual of words.	• I can always spell common words correctly. • I can spell all word lists accurately. • I can maintain accurate spelling of all but the most complex and unfamiliar words in all my writing.
Create opportunities for literary features.	• I can use more sophisticated similes in my writing, where appropriate. • I can use metaphors to describe, where it is effective, in my writing. (E.g. The car is a purring leopard on the road.) • I can use personification for effect to my writing. (E.g. The moon smiled with joy on the scene.)
Use a wider range of truly ambitious vocabulary (WOW words) appropriately and spelt correctly	• I can choose interesting vocabulary that is ambitious for my age, will engage the reader and is particularly appropriate for the writing task. • I can choose words and phrases to create deliberate effect in my writing. • I can make thoughtful vocabulary choices and justify my choices.

Natalie (Standard 7: Year 6)

Natalie's piece of writing requires very little improvement and it may only require a conversation with her to a) see if there was a reason she chose to print and b) re-enforce the necessity to always join unless there is a good reason not to. However, these targets can also, if necessary, be given as short term 'child speak' targets as follows:

Small step targets / Child speak targets
'Quick win' small step target: • All my writing in school is neat, accurate, and – when appropriate – joined.
'Quick win' small step target: • I can use a wide range of sophisticated connectives, linking words and sequence words correctly and confidently in my writing.

Oxford Writing Criterion Scale:

Progressive Skills Ladders and Child Speak Targets

Using the Child Speak Targets

The most effective way to ensure children make progress towards their medium term targets is to empower them through Assessment for Learning. This can be achieved through the setting of small step targets, linked to a progressive skills ladder.

On the following pages you will find Progressive Skills Ladders for each aspect of writing as follows:

- Handwriting
- Spelling
- Grammar and punctuation (including 'connectives')
- Vocabulary
- Length, detail and description (leading into 'writing voice')

The Skills Ladder for each aspect of writing is organised according to the expectations of the year group or key stage and describes the small steps – in a rough hierarchy – that some children will need to take in their progress towards security of each skill. These Skills Ladders should be used to guide target setting for individual children but should not be used rigidly, as a tick list. Children who make good progress will not need to take all of these small steps and some steps may be more or less relevant to individual children. Teachers will need to use their professional judgement and knowledge of each child in setting appropriate targets.

From Year 1/P2 onwards, each of the small steps is described in the form of a Child Speak Target. These can be given directly to children as part of the AfL process.

The process for setting small step targets is described in more detail on pages 50–52.

Handwriting

Name:		Date:	
Year/Key Stage	**Reference Number**	**Small step target / Child speak target (Year 1 onwards)**	**Secure skill? (✔, ✗)**
Reception (Pre-Writing) NB: These targets are not for sharing with the children in this form, but small aspects of a target may be given orally and in a non-stressful way.	H1	Can hold a pencil or crayon with enough control to make marks.	
	H2	Can sit correctly at a table.	
	H3	Can sit correctly at a table, holding a pencil comfortably and correctly.	
	H4	Can mark-make without help.	
	H5	Can make mark-making follow a pattern *(e.g. in a row or circle)*.	
	H6	Is trying to write letter shapes	
	H7	Can recognize own name within a group of others.	
	H8	Can copy over and under patterns and letters.	
	H9	Can use a favourite (preferred) hand when mark-making.	
	H10	Can sound the letters in own name.	
	H11	Can recognize and name all letter shapes. *(Can be further differentiated into even smaller steps by clustering small groups of like letters together.)*	
	H12	Can draw the first letter of their name.	
	H13	Is beginning to draw a range of recognizable letters.	
	H14	Can hold and use a pencil effectively to write letters.	
	H15	Knows writing goes from left to right in English.	
	H16	Is trying to write from left to right.	
Reception NB: These targets are not for sharing with the children in this form, but small aspects of a target may be given orally and in a non-stressful way.	H17	Can write their name.	
	H18	Can form most letters in the alphabet. *(More than 16)*	
	H19	Is beginning to write both capital letters and small case letters, saying which they are.	
	H20	Can form every letter of the alphabet.	
	H21	Can write some regular words, making the letters similar in size.	
	H22	Can usually write all letters the same size.	
	H23	Can copy adult sentences accurately, making writing regular in size.	
	H24	Can start most letters in the correct place. *(More than 16)*	
	H25	Is starting to put spaces between the words written.	
	H26	Can write all letters starting in the right place. *(Can be further differentiated into even smaller steps by clustering small groups of like letters together.)*	
	H27	Can form all letters correctly on the line, above the line and below the line. *(Ascenders / descenders)*	
	H28	Is beginning to write own sentences neatly and correctly.	

Handwriting

Name:		Date:	
Year/Key Stage	**Reference Number**	**Small step target / Child speak target (Year 1 onwards)**	**Secure skill? (✔, ✗)**
Year 1 From Year 1 onwards, the targets are presented as child speak targets for sharing with the children.	H29	I can write all letters accurately, starting and finishing in the right place. *(Can be further differentiated into even smaller steps by clustering small groups of like letters together.)*	
	H30	I can hold my pencil correctly.	
	H31	I sit correctly at the table when I am writing.	
	H32	I always use capital and small letters correctly. *(Upper/lower case)*	
	H33	I always have spaces between my words.	
	H34	I am starting to sit my writing on the line.	
	H35	I can draw sticks above the other letters and tails below the line of writing. (Ascenders/descenders)	
	H36	I can always write on the line, with ascenders showing clearly above small case letters and descenders below the line.	
	H37	I can maintain neat, well-formed writing for a paragraph or more.	
Year 2	H38	I am starting to join all my writing *(in accordance with the school's chosen style).*	
	H39	I can maintain accurate formation of all letters.	
	H40	I can maintain neat, regular writing for up to a side of A4 or more.	
Key Stage 2	H41	All my writing in school is neat, accurate, and – when appropriate – joined.	
	H42	I can use other fonts in my handwriting for emphasis or impact. *(E.g. capitalization, italic or 'ghost' writing.)*	

Spelling

Year/Key Stage	Reference Number	Small step target / Child speak target (Year 1 onwards)	Secure skill? (✔, ✗)
Name:		**Date:**	
Reception (Pre-Writing)	S1	Can recognize own name within others in a group. *(Oral and by pointing)*	
	S2	Can draw the first letter of their name.	
	S3	Can sound the letters in their name.	
	S4	Can spell their name out loud.	
	S5	Can write their name *(may not be quite spelt correctly)*. Letter size and shape may be irregular.	
Reception NB: These targets are not for sharing with the children in this form, but small aspects of a target may be given orally and in a non-stressful way.	S6	Can spell their first name correctly.	
	S7	Can spell some words on the Reception High Frequency Word Lists.	
	S8	Can sound most of the letters of the alphabet.	
	S9	Can name and sound all the letters of the alphabet	
	S10	Is beginning to use some phonic skills to write simple words. *(The teacher should record which the child uses.)*	
	S11	Usually spells C.V.C. words *(consonant, vowel, consonant)* correctly. *(This can be further differentiated by making targets for small sets of words at a time.)*	
	S12	Is starting to write CVC words. *(Should be phonically plausible.)*	
	S13	Is using all phonics *(taught so far)* to write simple words not known by sight.	
	S14	Can spell most CVC words correctly.	
	S15	Can spell CVC and CCVC, CVCC and CCVCC words using current phonic knowledge *(phase 4 Letters and Sounds or equivalent depending upon phonic programme being used)*. *(This can be further differentiated by making targets for small sets of words at a time.)*	
	S16	I can spell half of the words on the Reception High Frequency Word lists.	
Year 1 From Year 1 onwards, the targets are presented as child speak targets for sharing with the children.	S17	I can spell half or more of the words on the Reception High Frequency Word Lists	
	S18	I can spell all the words on the Reception High Frequency Word Lists.	
	S19	I can spell some words on the Year 1 High Frequency Word Lists.	
	S20	I can spell the common diagraphs.	
	S21	I always spell CVC words correctly.	
	S22	I can spell my own first and last name correctly.	
	S23	I can spell half or more of the words on the Year 1 portion of the Year 1 and 2 N.C. word lists and the Year 1 High Frequency Word List correctly. *(This can be further differentiated by making targets for small groups of words, for example four or six at a time.)*	
	S24	I can use phonics to make sensible efforts to spell words that I do not know by sight.	
	S25	I know all my phonics.	
	S26	I can spell all the words on the Year 1 portion of the Year 1 and 2 N.C. word lists and the Year 1 High Frequency Word List correctly.	

Spelling

Name:		Date:	
Year/Key Stage	**Reference Number**	**Small step target / Child speak target (Year 1 onwards)**	**Secure skill? (✔, ✘)**
Year 2	S27	I can always spell common single syllable words correctly. *(From the Reception and Years 1 and 2 High Frequency Word Lists and the Years 1 and 2 N.C. word lists).*	
	S28	I can spell some of the words from the Year 2 N.C. Word Lists and the High Frequency Word List for Year 2 correctly.	
	S29	I can use my phonics to help spell out harder words.	
	S30	I can use syllables to 'chop' up unknown words to support my spelling.	
	S31	I can maintain accurate spelling of words I know, in a side or more of A4 writing.	
	S32	I can spell all of the words from the Year 2 N.C. Word Lists and the High Frequency Word List for Year 2 correctly.	
Key Stage 2	S33	I can always spell common words correctly. *(From the Reception and Years 1 and 2 High Frequency Word Lists and the Years 1 and 2 N.C. Word lists.)*	
	S34	I can spell some of the words from Years 3 and 4, and 5 and 6 N.C. Word Lists and the High Frequency Word List for Years 4 and 5 correctly.	
	S35	I can use my phonics to help spell out harder words.	
	S36	I can use syllables to 'chop' up unknown words to support my spelling.	
	S37	I can maintain accurate spelling of words I know, in a side or more of A4 writing.	
	S38	I can always spell common words correctly. (From the Key Stage 2 N.C. Word Lists and the Years 4 and 5 High Frequency Word Lists.)	
	S39	I can spell all word lists accurately.	
	S40	I can maintain accurate spelling of all but the most complex and unfamiliar words in all my writing.	

Grammar and Punctuation (including 'Connectives')

NB: the reference number indicates whether the step is related to grammar (G), punctuation (P) or connectives (C). Some of these steps are also repeated in the vocabulary strand.

Year/Key Stage	Reference Number	Small step target / Child speak target (Year 1 onwards)	Secure skill? (✔, ✗)
Name:		**Date:**	
Reception NB: These targets are not for sharing with the children in this form, but small aspects of a target may be given orally and in a non-stressful way.	P1	Can point to full stops followed by capital letters in other people's writing.	
	P2	Can point to and name full stops and capital letters.	
	P3	Knows that there must always be a capital letter after a full stop.	
	P4	Can put a full stop on the end of a given sentence.	
	P5	Can put full stops into a short piece of writing that is understood.	
	P6	Can find all the full stops in a short piece of writing.	
	P7	Can put missing capital letters after the full stops in a short piece of writing.	
	G1 (V5)	Can talk correctly about things that have happened in the past.	
	G2 (V6)	Can talk correctly about things that are happening now.	
	G3 (V7)	Can talk correctly about things that might happen in the future.	
	C1	Can point to the word 'and' in short pieces of writing.	
	C2	Knows that 'and' is used to join things or simple sentences.	
	C3	Can point to 'but' and 'so' in writing. *(May be given individually as separate targets.)*	
	C4	Can use 'and', 'but' and 'so' in talk. *(May be given individually as separate targets.)*	
	C5	Can use 'and' in own writing.	
	C6 (V8)	Can use connectives such as 'and', 'but', 'so' and 'then' in talk.	
Year 1 From Year 1 onwards, the targets are presented as child speak targets for sharing with the children.	P8	I am beginning to use full stops and capital letters to show where sentences begin and end in my writing.	
	P9	I know what a question mark looks like.	
	P10	I can use some full stops and capital letters to show most sentences in my writing.	
	P11	I can point to question marks in writing.	
	P12	I can usually use full stops and capital letters to show sentences in my writing.	
	P13	I can tell which sentences are questions.	
	P14	I can change my voice for a question mark in reading.	
	P15	I can draw question marks on the ends of questions.	
	P16	I can point to commas in writing.	
	P17	I always use full stops and capital letters accurately to show sentences in my writing.	
	P18	I am beginning to use questions marks in my writing.	
	P19	I am beginning to use commas in my writing.	
	P20	I can use capital 'I' consistently, to name myself.	
	P21	I use a capital letter to start the word, when writing someone's name.	

Grammar and Punctuation (including 'Connectives')

Name:		Date:	
Year/Key Stage	**Reference Number**	**Small step target / Child speak target (Year 1 onwards)**	**Secure skill? (✔, ✗)**
Year 1 (cont.) From Year 1 onwards, the targets are presented as child speak targets for sharing with the children.	G4	I can talk correctly in Standard English.	
	G5 (V18)	I am starting to use descriptive noun phrases in my talk. *(E.g. The tired, old man… a small, white dog…)*	
	C7	I can use simple sequence words in my writing. *(E.g. First, then, next, last, before, after, etc.)*	
	C8	I can use 'and', 'but' and 'so' to join simple sentences.	
	C9	I can use a wider range of connectives in my writing. *(E.g. but, so, and, then, etc.)*	
	C10	I am trying to use simple linking words and phrases in my writing. *(E.g. after, before, then, soon, at last, etc.)*	
	C11	I am trying to use one or two of the first Year 2 connectives in my writing. *(E.g. or, if, when, because, as, although, etc.)*	
	C12	I can sometimes start a sentence with a connective.	
Year 2	P22	I can usually use question marks in my writing, when they are needed.	
	P23	I can point to and name exclamation marks in writing.	
	P24	I can change my voice for an exclamation mark in reading.	
	P25	I can help to put commas between things in a list in written sentences.	
	P26	I can put exclamation marks on the end of simple exclamations.	
	P27	I can always use full stops, question marks and capitals correctly to show sentences.	
	P28	I can usually use exclamation marks in the right place in my writing.	
	P29	I can point to apostrophes in a piece of writing. (Singular possession and simple contraction only at Key Stage 1.)	
	P30	I am beginning to use commas in my writing.	
	P31	I can put commas in the correct places in given sentences.	
	P32	I can use apostrophes *(for singular possession)* in given sentences.	
	P33	I can always use full stops, capital letters, question marks and exclamation marks correctly in my writing.	
	P34	I can usually use commas for lists correctly in my writing.	
	P35	I am beginning to use apostrophes *(for singular possession)* correctly in my writing.	
	P36	I can use apostrophes to show ownership *(e.g. the dog's bone)*.	
	P37	I can use commas correctly for lists in my writing.	
	P38	I can use apostrophes *(for singular possession)* correctly in my writing.	
	P39	I can use apostrophes *(for simple contractions)* in given sentences.	
	P40	I am beginning to use apostrophes for simple contractions correctly in my writing.	
	P41	I can use apostrophes for simple contractions correctly in my writing.	
	G6 (V23)	I can use noun phrases to describe things in my writing. *(E.g. The tired, old man…)*	
	G7 (V28)	I can use time and sequence words to link parts of my sentences when they are needed. *(E.g. Before, after, next, later, yesterday, tomorrow, etc.) (This can be further differentiated by targeting each form individually.)*	
	G8 (V29)	I can start my sentences in different ways, such as with 'ly' words, 'ing' words and connectives, time and sequence words, prepositions *(e.g. Under… Beside… Above… Below…)* etc. *(This can be further differentiated by targeting each form individually.)*	

Grammar and Punctuation (including 'Connectives')

Name:		Date:	
Year/Key Stage	**Reference Number**	**Small step target / Child speak target (Year 1 onwards)**	**Secure skill? (✔, ✗)**
Year 2 (cont.)	C13	I can use a range of connectives in my writing. (E.g. or, if, when, because, as, although, etc.)	
	C14 (V27)	I can use a wider range of connectives, such as: 'when', 'if', 'because', 'as', 'as well as' and 'although' in my talk and in my writing, when they are needed.	
	C15	I can use a range of linking and sequence words. (E.g. before, after, later, next, also, after a while, at the same time, one day, Last week, etc.)	
	C16	I can use a range of connectives to open sentences in my writing. (E.g. If… When… Because…)	
	C17	I try not to use the same connective too often.	
Key Stage 2	P42	I can use all KS1 punctuation accurately (. ! ? , ').	
	P43	I can use commas after fronted adverbials.	
	P44	I can name ellipsis, hyphen, dashes and speech marks correctly. (May be given each as a separate target)	
	P45	I can put all the following punctuation into a given piece of writing: . ! ? , ' … - " "	
	P46	I can use inverted commas (speech marks) to show direct speech.	
	P47	I can use all the following punctuation in my own writing, mainly accurately: . ! ? , ' … - " "	
	P48	I can name brackets, semi-colon and colon correctly. (This can be further differentiated by targeting each one individually.)	
	P49	I can accurately punctuate direct speech.	
	P50	I can use a colon to introduce a list.	
	P51	I can use appropriate punctuation to show parenthesis. (() - - , ,)	
	P52	I can use semi colons to mark boundaries between independent clauses.	
	P53	I can use dashes to mark boundaries between independent clauses.	
	P54	I can use colons to mark boundaries between independent clauses.	
	P55	I can use the following range of punctuation in my own writing, mainly accurately, when appropriate: . ! ? , ' … - " " ( ) ; :	
	P56	I can use punctuation for effect or impact.	
	P57	I can use punctuation appropriately for purpose in lists, including the colon and semi-colons.	
	P58	I use the full range of punctuation appropriately and accurately.	
	G9 (V40)	I can use a wide range of ways to start sentences.	
	G10 (V41)	I can use the passive voice in writing. (E.g. That cake was eaten by the child.)	
	C18	I can use more sophisticated connectives in my writing. (E.g. although, however, nevertheless, as well as, despite, contrary to, in spite of, etc.)	
	C19	I can use more sophisticated links and sequence phrases in my writing. (E.g. eventually, as a result of, in addition to, in spite of, as well as, a little while later, soon after that, since, etc.)	
	C20	I can use more sophisticated connectives to open sentences in my writing. (E.g. Although…, However…, Despite…, Contrary to…)	
	C21	I can use sophisticated connectives and links within sentences and to open sentences in my writing. (E.g. In addition to…, As if…, Nevertheless…, Despite…, Contrary to…, Eventually…, Consequently…, Subsequently…, Referring back to…, In anticipation of…, etc.)	
	C22	I can use a wide range of sophisticated connectives, linking words and sequence words correctly and confidently in my writing.	

Ambitious Vocabulary

NB: Includes both the use of ambitious words and ambitious use of ambitious words.

Year/Key Stage	Reference Number	Small step target / Child speak target (Year 1 onwards)	Secure skill? (✔, ✗)
Name:		**Date:**	
Reception These targets are not for sharing with the children in this form, but small aspects of a target may be given orally and in a non-stressful way.	V1	Can speak clearly and confidently.	
	V2	Enjoys learning new words and using them when explaining their thinking.	
	V3	Knows some 'WOW' words.	
	V4	Can describe how they are doing something.	
	V5 (G1)	Can talk correctly about things that have happened in the past.	
	V6 (G2)	Can talk correctly about things that are happening now.	
	V7 (G3)	Can talk correctly about things that might happen in the future.	
	V8 (C6)	Can use connectives such as 'and', 'but', 'so' and 'then' in talk.	
	V9	Can use simple adjectives for description in talk.	
	V10	Can use simple adverbs for description in talk.	
Year 1 From Year 1 onwards, the targets are presented as child speak targets for sharing with the children.	V11	I can usually guess the meaning of words I do not know from the sense of the story.	
	V12	I understand and am using connectives such as 'when', 'if', 'because' and 'as' in my sentences.	
	V13	I am trying to use a lot of different words in my talk and in my writing.	
	V14	I can make suitable word choices from the 'wow' word wall, word banks, etc.	
	V15	I can use 'WOW' words in my talk.	
	V16	I can use adjectives in my writing.	
	V17	I can use adverbs in my writing.	
	V18 (G5)	I am starting to use descriptive noun phrases in my talk. (E.g. The tired, old man… a small, white dog…)	
	V19	I can use 'ly' words, 'ing' words and connectives in VCOP games and activities.	

Ambitious Vocabulary

Name:		Date:	
Year/Key Stage	**Reference Number**	**Small step target / Child speak target (Year 1 onwards)**	**Secure skill? (✔, ✗)**
Year 2	V20	I can use interesting adjectives and adverbs in short pieces of writing.	
	V21	I can use 'ly' words, 'ing' words and connectives to start my sentences in talk and writing.	
	V22	I am using a lot of 'WOW' words in talk and am starting to use them in writing, usually correctly.	
	V23 (G6)	I can use noun phrases to describe things in my writing. *(E.g. The tired, old man…)*	
	V24	I can use interesting and effective adjectives to describe things.	
	V25	I can use interesting and effective adverbs to describe actions.	
	V26	I can begin to use similes to describe and compare things. *(E.g. The dog is as big as an elephant.)*	
	V27 (C14)	I can use a wider range of connectives, such as: 'when', 'if', 'because', 'as', 'as well as' and 'although' in my talk and in my writing, when they are needed.	
	V28 (G7)	I can use time and sequence words to link parts of my sentences when they are needed. *(E.g. Before, after, next, later, yesterday, tomorrow, etc.) (This can be further differentiated by targeting each form individually.)*	
	V29 (G8)	I can start my sentences in different ways, such as with 'ly' words, 'ing' words and connectives, time and sequence words, prepositions *(e.g. Under… Beside… Above… Below…)* etc. *(This can be further differentiated by targeting each form individually.)*	
	V30	I can use a range of 'WOW' words (ambitious vocabulary) in my writing.	
Key Stage 2	V31	I can use a wide range of vocabulary that is ambitious for my age, correctly in my writing.	
	V32	I can choose interesting vocabulary that is ambitious for my age, will engage the reader and is particularly appropriate for the writing task.	
	V33	I can choose words and phrases to create deliberate effect in my writing.	
	V34	I can make thoughtful vocabulary choices and justify my choices.	
	V35	I am starting to use truly sophisticated vocabulary in my writing.	
	V36	I am able to paint vivid descriptions in my writing, when they are needed.	
	V37	I can use more sophisticated similes in my writing, where appropriate.	
	V38	I can use metaphors to describe, where it is effective, in my writing. *(E.g. The car is a purring leopard on the road.)*	
	V39	I can use personification for effect to my writing. *(E.g. The moon smiled with joy on the scene.)*	
	V40 (G9)	I can use a wide range of ways to start sentences.	
	V41 (G10)	I can use the passive voice in my writing. *(E.g. That cake was eaten by the child.)*	
	V42	I can use truly sophisticated vocabulary in my writing, when it is needed.	
	V43	I can use technical and specific vocabulary which is matched to the purpose and audience of my writing.	
	V44	I can discuss and justify how word choice can alter the meaning and effect of writing.	
	V45	My writing is lively, varied and sophisticated.	

Length, Detail and Description developing into 'Writing Voice'

Name:		Date:	
Year/Key Stage	**Reference Number**	**Small step target / Child speak target (Year 1 onwards)**	**Secure skill? (✔, ✗)**
Reception These targets are not for sharing with the children in this form, but small aspects of a target may be given orally and in a non-stressful way.	LDD1	Is learning a wide range of words.	
	LDD2	Is speaking in full sentences.	
	LDD3	Is beginning to join simple sentences to make longer ones.	
	LDD4	Is beginning to add simple descriptions.	
	LDD5	Is starting to write simple sentences, labels, titles or other text. *(May be copying other's writing.)*	
	LDD6	Can write three simple sentences or more on the same subject.	
	LDD7	Is beginning to join simple sentences together in writing, using at least 'and' or 'but'.	
	LDD8	Is starting to write more than one sentence about the same thing or idea.	
Year 1 From Year 1 onwards, the targets are presented as child speak targets for sharing with the children.	LDD9	I am beginning to write my own ideas so that others can read and understand them.	
	LDD10	I am beginning to write simple stories, news, reports, retell, labels and lists. *(May be broken down into separate targets.)*	
	LDD11	I can use a simple structure in my story writing – beginning, middle, end.	
	LDD12	I can use simple adjectives in writing for detail and interest. *(May be given individually as separate targets.)*	
	LDD13	I can use simple adverbs in writing for detail and interest. *(May be given individually as separate targets.)*	
	LDD14	I can write at least a paragraph on a subject.	
Year 2	LDD15	I can start sentences in different ways.	
	LDD16	I can use a wider range of connectives to join sentences, e.g. 'and', 'but', 'so', 'then'. *(May be given individually as separate targets.)*	
	LDD17	I can use a wider range of adjectives and adverbs appropriately. *(May be given individually as separate targets.)*	
	LDD18	I can use simple sequence and time links *(e.g. first, next, last, after, before, etc.)*.	
	LDD19	I can use any 3 'w' words to increase length and detail *(when, where, who, what, why plus how)*.	
	LDD20	I can write a longer piece of writing. *(Close to a side of A4.)*	
	LDD21	I am beginning to use a wider range of connectives, e.g. 'when', 'if', 'because', 'as', 'although'. *(May be given individually as separate targets.)*	
	LDD22	I can use adjectives, adverbs and descriptive noun phrases to add detail in writing. *(May be given individually as separate targets.)*	
	LDD23	I can write about at least 3 of the 5 key elements + 'how' to provide detail in sections of my writing (who, what, where, when, why + how) when appropriate.	
	LDD24	I can organize my writing to reflect the type of writing I am doing, such as using the features of instructions.	

Oxford Primary Writing Assessment

Length, Detail and Description developing into 'Writing Voice'

Name:		Date:	
Year/Key Stage	**Reference Number**	**Small step target / Child speak target (Year 1 onwards)**	**Secure skill? (✔, ✗)**
Key Stage 2	LDD25	I can write a longer piece with an opening, a body and an ending, that has at least 3 of the 5 key elements, *(who, what, where, when, why + how)* in each part.	
	LDD26	I can stop and describe at least one of the key elements (who, what, where, when, why + how) in each section of writing.	
	LDD27	I am beginning to use direct speech in my writing.	
	LDD28	I am beginning to organize my sections into paragraphs in writing.	
	LDD29	My writing is usually lively and interesting with length, detail and description.	
	LDD30	I can use paragraphs to signpost the beginning, middle and end of a story.	
	LDD31	I can use paragraphs to show a change in setting in a story.	
	LDD32	I can use paragraphs to show a change of time in a story.	
	LDD33	I can use paragraphs to show a change of action in a story.	
	LDD34	I can move down a line when someone starts to speak.	
	LDD35	I can group similar information together into paragraphs in non-fiction writing.	
	LDD36	I can open my paragraphs by signposting what may happen next.	
	LDD37	I can open my paragraphs with links back to something that happened previously.	
	LDD38	I can open paragraphs by signalling changes in time to guide the reader through the text.	
	LDD39	I can use paragraphs to structure a story into opening, build-up, problem, resolution and ending.	
	LDD40	I can use connectives within paragraphs to link ideas and sentences. *(E.g. As soon as…, Despite that…, Contrary to her saying that she…, etc.)*	
	LDD41	In narrative, I can refer back to an event at the beginning that can affect the ending.	
	LDD42	I can vary the length of sentences or paragraphs to affect the reader.	
	LDD43	I can use direct speech accurately most of the time.	
	LDD44	I can always use paragraphs accurately	
	LDD45	I am beginning to use a good range of organizational devices *(e.g. sub-headings, lists, bullets, brackets, direct speech, etc.)* as appropriate to text type.	
	LDD46	In non-fiction writing, I can write a clear introduction, followed by logical points, closing with a clear conclusion.	
	LDD47	My writing is always lively and interesting with good length, detail and description.	
	LDD48	I can use most organizational features correctly.	
	LDD49	I can use a wide range of ways to open sentences, including using 'ly' words, 'ing' words and connectives.	
	LDD50	My writing is always well organized, using a wide range of organizational and literary devices accurately and appropriately *(e.g. passive voice, simile, metaphor, onomatopoeia, alliteration, etc.). (May be given individually as separate targets.)*	
	LDD51	I can use sentences of different length for effect.	
	LDD52	I can use parenthesis for style and effect *(brackets, double dash and double commas).*	

Length, Detail and Description developing into 'Writing Voice'

Name:		Date:	
Year/Key Stage	**Reference Number**	**Small step target / Child speak target (Year 1 onwards)**	**Secure skill? (✔, ✗)**
Key Stage 2 (cont)	LDD53	I can use dialogue confidently and accurately.	
	LDD54	I can use the full range of organizational devices such as paragraphs, sub headings, footnotes, bullets, contents and bibliographies, to help the reader.	
	LDD55	I can use power features confidently and accurately. *('ly' words, 'ing' words and connectives, sophisticated 'WOW' words and ?! . . .).*	
	LDD56	I show good awareness of the audience when appropriate. *(E.g. Asides, additional detail, justification, explanation, etc.)*	
	LDD57	I can open and conclude my writing in different and sometimes unexpected ways.	

Skills Progression for Big Writing

Schools who follow the *Big Writing* approach, or schools who would prefer to see the strands for writing grouped by individual skill, may wish to use the skills progression ladders and associated child speak targets on pages 137–140 rather than the amalgamated 'Grammar and punctuation (including connectives)' above. The *Big Writing* Punctuation and Connectives pyramids have been updated in line with National Expectations and are also included on pages 141–142.

Reporting Pupil Attainment and Progress

All schools are accountable for the attainment and progress that their children make and are required to provide evidence of such at various points and to various stakeholders.

One of the challenges for teachers in England, following the removal of NC Levels and 'average points progress' is how to report the attainment and progress of pupils in a consistent way, and in a way which a range of stakeholders will understand. In truth, the system of Levels, Sub-Levels and Points has led to a focus on numbers and data that, for the most part, are fairly meaningless. Their removal presents a genuine opportunity for schools to focus on the evidence that matters and to use assessment for formative purposes so that, rather than just 'weighing and measuring' pupils occasionally and filling in spreadsheets for accountability purposes, teachers and children are equipped with the knowledge to make progress and attainment actually happen.

Numerical data tracking

As has already been shown (pages 8–9), the Oxford Writing Criterion Scale can help with reporting attainment and progress in a simple 'numerical' way for the purposes of termly, top level data capture and analysis. On the OWCS – in line with the 2014 National Curriculum – children are expected to make a year's progress in a year. So, for example, a child might progress from a Standard 2 Secure at the end of Year 1/P2 to a Standard 3 Secure by the end of Year 2/P3.

That said, it is important to note that the Developing, Secure and Advanced categories on the OWCS are not 'equal thirds' of a year. The Developing and Advanced categories are deliberately narrow because they serve as entry and exit points, whilst the Secure category is broad, identifying those children who are good writers for their age but still in the process of honing some skills.

Thus, if we assume a school year to be 36 weeks, a typical child might be expected to track the OWCS Standard for their year group as follows:

Developing	Secure	Advanced
6 weeks	24 weeks	6 weeks

Of course, real children aren't like this and real progress will be more erratic for all manner of reasons. Plus schools following the principles of the mastery curriculum will want to encourage children to progress by broadening and deepening their knowledge and skills and applying them to a range of contexts – rather than always moving 'on' with new learning. Generally speaking, as long as a child progresses from Developing (by end of autumn term) to Secure (by end of summer term) they will have made almost a year's progress and should remain on track to meet national expectations. The following year, the same child might make more progress; things tend to balance out across a Key Stage. However, if progress starts to slow the teacher would want to investigate further.

It goes without saying that children who are behind expectations in terms of attainment will need to make far more than a year's progress in a year if they are to catch up – although they also need to 'secure' their skills along the way if they are not to lose them again later on. Likewise, high achievers whose progress stalls will be cause for concern even if they remain on track to meet the end of Key Stage National Standard; National Standard is not suitably ambitious for these children and where schools are held to account on progress this will be noticed, unless there is qualitative evidence (see page 73) of depth and mastery in their writing across the curriculum.

Attainment and progress at Cravenwood Academy, Manchester

Below is the genuine tracking of a sample of Year 6 pupils from a newly opened Academy in the Manchester area. These pupils were 'baseline' assessed in September and assessed again at the end of every term.

Name	Sept 2014	Dec 2014	March 2015	July 2015	Commentary
Zinedine	6-D	6-S	6-S	7-S	This child has made more than a year's progress and is on track to meet the high expectations of the curriculum
Zara	5-S	Abs	6-D/S	6-S	This child has made a year's progress; she is slightly behind the high expectations of the new curriculum but may achieve National Standard (if this were 2016)
Sumaiya	4-S	5-D	5-S	7-D	This child has made exceptional progress – almost 3 years in 1 year! She is close to meeting the high expectations of the curriculum
Madeeha	4-S	5-S	4-A	5-S	This child's progress was erratic through the year but overall she achieved a year's progress. She remains behind the high expectations of the new curriculum (though on track to achieve a Level 4 or above in 2015)
Ahmad	3-D	3-S	3-A	4-S	This child is well behind expectations but has made over a year's progress.
Iram	2-A	3-S	3-S	4-S	This child is well behind expectations but has made exceptional progress – almost 2 years in 1 year.

As well as being an example of what tracking across a cohort of children might look like, this chart reflects the impact of linking the OWCS to clear target setting and quality teaching through *Big Writing*. Cravenwood Academy was created from a school in difficult circumstances and had some children who were significantly behind in their writing and/or labelled as having a special educational need in writing. Ros Wilson worked with this school to review and moderate writing assessments, ensure that the evidence was translated into clear targets for pupils, and train all staff in the *Big Writing* approach.

High expectations are also vital. Some teachers might have been tempted to 'write Iram off' given his very low Standard for an eleven year old. In fact, he achieves a Secure Standard 4, which is a very functional Standard for daily life and gives him a fighting chance of success at secondary school.

An example class tracking sheet is provided on page 13 (and online at www.oxfordowl.co.uk).

What to do with the data?

The simple system described above enables any interested party – class teachers, senior leaders, governors and inspectors – to see, at a glance, the attainment and progress of pupils. This is valuable for accountability purposes but the most important thing is the analysis of the data.

The assessment or subject lead – and/or a member of the senior leadership team or governors – will want to review the data across each class and across the whole school to ascertain trends or areas of need. Here are some things to consider when looking at the data:

Oxford Primary Writing Assessment

Analysis	Next steps
All pupils are attaining and moving forward at the expected rate in writing or better. Has any particular group made accelerated progress? (You may want to look at the data by e.g. gender, FSM, Pupil Premium, DOB.)	• Celebrate this achievement and encourage it to continue - or preferably, be even greater next time! • You may also want to analyse what's working so well so that you can maintain this approach. • Consider some action research or writing a case study so that you can share your experiences with other schools.

Some children have not made much progress – or significantly less progress than expected or required (e.g. for a child already below expectations)
 	
One or more children have made no progress at all – or may even have dropped back
	• Review the most recent and previous OWCS assessments for each child. Are they accurate? Re-assess just to be sure and adjust data if needed.
	• Review the medium term targets (see pages xx-xx) set at the previous assessment. Is there any evidence of achievement against these?
	• Have a conversation with the class teacher, comparing the two assessments and discussing your conclusions
	  - Listen to and discuss explanations
	  - Look for solutions not excuses
	  - Plan for appropriate action or intervention based on the specific needs identified

Has any class made significantly more progress than other classes?	• Review the two previous OWCS assessments as described above. Are they accurate? • Scrutinise children's writing books or portfolios and outcomes of the weekly Big Write. Are the assessment outcomes supported by wider evidence? • If the above are secure, have a conversation with the class teacher to identify any reasons / additional strategies he or she thinks may have impacted on children's attainment and progress. • If appropriate, observe the teacher in the oral session for Big Writing. • Consider videoing this teacher for CPD purposes or having other staff observe their lessons. • If appropriate, is this teacher a potential co-driver for Big Writing?

Has any class made significantly less progress than other classes?	• Review the two previous OWCS assessments as described above. Are they accurate?
	• Scrutinise children's writing books or portfolios and outcomes of the weekly Big Write. Examine:
	  - Evidence of progress from week to week
	  - Quality of marking and feedback to children
	  - Evidence of use of appropriate short term / small tep targets
	  - Evidence of pupil involvement in AfL
	  - Evidence of pupil editing and up-levelling.
	• Draw your conclusions and discuss with the senior management team.
	• Have a conversation with the teacher, discussing all that you have seen / examined:
	  - Listen to explanations
	  - Plan appropriate support and CPD for the teacher
	  - Plan action or intervention for pupils as required

Has any particular group made significantly less progress than others?
(You may want to look at the data by e.g. gender, FSM, Pupil Premium, DOB.)
	• Conduct a review of the OWCS assessments and writing portfolios as above. Is the evidence accurate and secure?
	• Have a conversation as a senior management team to discuss possible explanations and solutions. Ask:
	  - Are we setting high enough expectations for these pupils?
	  - Does the teaching programme or timetable need adjusting to suit the needs of these pupils?
	  - Is there a staff training issue?
	• Have a discussion with the whole staff, briefing on any concerns and listening to explanations
	• Plan appropriate support and CPD for staff
	• Plan action or intervention for pupils

Qualitative evidence of progress

Whilst the numerical data shown on page 71 provides a useful overview, it doesn't give an accurate picture of what each child's writing actually looks like! And it doesn't give any information about what that child can do and what they need to do next; it is only a child's individual OWCS that will do this. This detailed evidence is needed to inform target setting (see pages 50–55) and teaching, to ensure that skills are secured and mastered and progress is made at the appropriate pace.

By far the best and clearest way of providing qualitative evidence of attainment and progress is through a portfolio of children's writing. This doesn't need to be a huge file but should include the three (or four if a September baseline is carried out) formally assessed pieces each year plus a selection of other writing from across the curriculum that provides evidence of children applying and developing new skills. It could also – if held electronically – include video evidence of children performing poetry or plays they have written, holding debates, orally persuading etc.

Similarly, the numerical data is not terribly useful for parents – other than giving them a sense of where there child is in relation to national expectations. Although, of course, this needs explaining!

It is not recommended that the numerical data is shared with children and teachers will certainly want to avoid 'labelling' children. That said, most children know whether they are good or not so good at something so it is really important that all children have goals, believe in their goals, and know exactly what they need to do to get there.

On the following page there is an example of a termly report to parents showing how a child's achievement and progress might be communicated. A blank template is provided on page 75 (or online at Oxford Owl).

Oxford Primary Writing Assessment

Pupil Progress Report: WRITING

Name: Sam Peters	DOB: 12/6/2008	Class: Maple, Year 2

Spring Term Report: 30th March 2015

Autumn Term: Standard 3 (Developing)	Spring Term: Standard 3 (Secure)	Summer Term:

Summary
Sam has been assessed as a Secure Standard 3 on the Oxford Writing Criterion Scale.
This means Sam is well on track to meet the standard required by the end of Year 2.
His effort and attention in class has improved enormously and he should feel really proud of
his progress in writing this term. Well done Sam!

Sam's strengths as a writer	• Good at communicating his ideas and putting details in his writing • Can write a range of different texts such as stories, letters, simple reports • Can structure sentences clearly, using good descriptive language • Good at spelling and uses phonics effectively to attempt the spelling of difficult words • Generally accurate with the punctuation that he knows (full stops, capital letters, ?) • Excellent handwriting, beginning to used joined writing

What Sam needs to focus on next	• Varying the structure of his sentences, for example:
	  - Using questions or exclamations occasionally
	  - Including dialogue in his writing
	  - Joining simple sentences together to make longer sentences using words such as: and, but, so, then, if
	• Using past and present tense correctly
	• Trying to make his writing more lively and interesting, for example by:
	  - Adding a little humour
	  - Experimenting with unusual words
	  - Extending descriptions using adjectives and adverbs

Things you could do to help Sam	Sam is good at the mechanics of writing – his spelling and handwriting is very good for a child his age. Sam now needs to work on the quality of his writing – and on interesting the reader. Spend time talking to Sam, asking him questions and encouraging him to extend his responses and give more detailed descriptions when he talks. Encourage Sam to notice the range of sentence structures in his reading – use of questions, exclamations and speech.

In this school we use the Oxford Writing Criterion Scale to assess children's writing once a term. It tells us exactly what each child can do, what they need to do next, and whether they are on track to meet nationally expected standards at the end of each Key Stage.

The Oxford Writing Criterion Scale is divided into seven 'Standards' – one for each year of primary school. Within each Standard children may be assessed as Developing, Secure or Advanced.

Below is a guide to where children should be at the end of each year. It is important to remember children learn and progress at different rates.

End YR	End Y1	End Y2	End Y3	End Y4	End Y5	End Y6
1S	2S	3S	4D/S	5D/S	6D/S	7D/S
Secure Standard 1	Secure Standard 2	Secure Standard 3	Developing or Secure Standard 4	Developing or Secure Standard 5	Developing or Secure Standard 6	Developing or Secure Standard 7

74

Pupil Progress Report: WRITING

Name:	DOB:	Class:

Achievement and progress in WRITING **TERM:**		
Autumn Term:	**Spring Term:**	**Summer Term:**

Summary	
Your child's strengths as a writer	
What your child needs to focus on next	
Things you could do to help your child	

In this school we use the Oxford Writing Criterion Scale to assess children's writing once a term. It tells us exactly what each child can do, what they need to do next, and whether they are on track to meet nationally expected standards at the end of each Key Stage.

The Oxford Writing Criterion Scale is divided into seven 'Standards' – one for each year of primary school. Within each Standard children may be assessed as Developing, Secure or Advanced.

Below is a guide to where children should be at the end of each year. However, it is important to remember children learn and progress at different rates.

End YR	End Y1	End Y2	End Y3	End Y4	End Y5	End Y6
1S	2S	3S	4D/S	5D/S	6D/S	7D/S
Secure Standard 1	Secure Standard 2	Secure Standard 3	Developing or Secure Standard 4	Developing or Secure Standard 5	Developing or Secure Standard 6	Developing or Secure Standard 7

Stimuli for Writing Assessment Tasks

Setting appropriate stimuli for writing is essential for achieving successful writing outcomes and undertaking meaningful assessment. Letters are a particularly useful text type for assessment purposes because they enable secure judgements on a wide range of features, such as organization and awareness of the audience. For those children working at higher expectations, letters can easily accommodate other text types within them to form hybrid texts, for example a letter with a set of embedded instructions or an excerpt from a newspaper report.

Although it is useful for all children to write to the same text type, it is important to offer them a selection of different stimuli, to enable them to choose the topic or theme they feel most motivated by and that will, therefore, enable them to produce their best writing.

The following list of example stimuli for writing letters are grouped into broad themes and are appropriate for all age groups, although some include suggested adaptations for older or younger children.

Friends, family and pets

1. Write a letter to a friend to tell them about what you did in the holidays/after school/at the weekend.

2. Write a letter to your mum or another family member or friend sent from space, to tell them that you have been kidnapped by aliens.

3. Write a letter to a friend about your life on another planet.

4. Write a letter from a dog, explaining how they feel about cats in the neighbourhood.

5. Write a letter to a potential buyer to persuade them to buy your house (or a fictional house) – include descriptive writing and/or the estate agent's details within the letter.

6. Write a letter to a friend giving them instructions for how to care for your pet (real or make-believe) while you are on holiday. As well as basic care instructions, your friend will need to know you pet's likes and dislikes, habits, fears and any strange or unique tendencies.

Fictional characters

1. Write a letter to Lord Voldemort/another evil fictional character (or a naughty story character, such as Goldilocks, for younger children) including a set of instructions on how to make people respect/like you.

2. Write a letter to Spiderman (or another superhero) thanking him for rescuing you. Include a text box with a short newspaper report on the rescue (for older children).

3. Write a letter in role as a ghost explaining why you are haunting the school or a local building OR write a letter to a ghost asking why they are haunting the school or a local building. Describe some of the things people have seen/heard in an embedded newspaper report (for older children).

4. Write a letter to a friend to tell them about the discovery you made of a tiny dinosaur/fairy/other make-believe creature in the woods/park/your garden.

5. Write a letter to tell Mrs Locks what Goldy has been getting up to in the home of the three bears.

Famous people

1. Write a letter to Prince Charles discussing whether he or his son, Prince William, should be the next king. (For younger children, write the letter to the Queen in 'Snow White' discussing who should rule – her or Snow White.)

2. Write a letter to the Prime Minister to tell him why your school is the best school in the country.

3. Write a letter to an author suggesting additional ideas that they could add to an already published story that the children have enjoyed (the letter could include an example of narrative to give the author a taster).

4. Write a letter to a famous person, asking them to visit your school. You will have to persuade them very convincingly as they get thousands of letters every day.

School/Local community

1. Write a letter to the Head Teacher telling her (persuading for older children) why he/she should close the school at lunch time each day.

2. Write a letter to the school's cook telling him/her what you think about school dinners – what you like and what you think could be improved and why.

3. Write a letter to a potential new teacher, persuading them to come and teach at your school by telling them all the wonderful things about the school.

4. Write a letter to the school governors, telling them what you like about your school and what you think could be improved.

5. Write a letter to the council complaining about traffic/litter/another local issue.

6. Write a letter to a fast food chain, complaining about the amount of packaging their food is served in.

7. Write a letter to a TV production company, to pitch an idea for a new reality show for children.

Un-assessed Writing Samples

The following un-assessed samples of children's writing have been provided for staff assessment and moderation tasks. There is an example for each Standard of the Oxford Writing Criterion Scale, although they are not arranged in any particular order. Judgements and assessor commentary for these samples can be found in Appendix 2 (pages 110–117).

Usman

Dear Mulan,
I am writing to say well done
from Saving China with mushu.
now you can put your feet
up and our topic is China. also
my favroit bit was making
Lanterns.
Oh and did you servive
the wor you must be very
proud and exorsed.
Usman

Billy

Dear Santa,

Spider man and DVD

billy

Love,

Billy

Anya

Monday 9ᵗʰ March 2015

Dear Elsa,

I am writting to tell you about what fantastic World book day I had! Firstly I dressed up as you and my dress kept lighting up, and I read a book about you and Anna, it was fantastic!

On world book day every body dressed up as their favroute Charecter, and me and Harley dressed up the Same. My wish is that I can meet you and, if I can go on an adventure to see princes Anna, and you.

My favroute part of the frozen book was when the gates of Anendelle were open and when Anna falls in love with Hans and he was about to become prince but you found out that he was evil. However the Sad bit was when the King and queen went on a boat and on a Stormy night it was very windy and the boat was sucked in a big wave.

I shared my book with Ameana and she even liked the book, but she didn't like it more than me. After that it was dinner time and when I went out I Seen that so many people were dressed up as you! when we came back we got some tokens from miss Smart.

My dress was glimmering every time I walked.
The glitter kept flickering on my dress and
when I sat down the glitter kept falling on
my chair and them my chair had a world
book day too!

Frantielly my hair kept coming out and it was
really annoying and even when I went home my dad
said to me why is your hair friezey and I said
because I had to two ponys on the side.

Smiling I had a when I got home I told
my mum what a brilliant day I had. She
replied thats amazing and I am happy you
enjoyed it. This year was the best world
book day I had yet!

PS: I just wish to go on an adventure with
you and you are my favroute character I
have ever heard and seen of. Thank you!

Your sincerly,

Anya

Jo

to mumee
I clihemd up
A been-stor.
A casl and.
I went-unto.
A casl then.
I sor sum
food

love Jo

love

Ryan

Dear Dom
I am writing too tell you abowt the beast trip ever we went to studio skills academy. It was exstrodenery, we made our own report. I was writing to ask if you can perswade youre teacher if you can go. It is the greatist thing ever! I thinck you woude love it. But show this letter two the teacher

there adots of instructions and lots of them you wil need. before you go on this trip You must spit youre class in two 4 team each person will get a special role here is whot you coude be.

Roles

producer
a producer is the one who is incharge of everything. if eney thing gose wrong it is up to him to sort everything

Director
the director is the one that is in controll of were they stand. and they say tape one

camora operator
The camora operator (camora man) is the one who films youre vidios.

from Ryan.

James

Wednesday 2ⁿᵈ April 2014

Barcelona,
Spain
SbMC68

Dear Finnley,

I am writing to you to inform you about our fantastic trip to the Living Rainforest.

Firstly, we walked excitedly into the Living Rainforest, and listened to the tour guide. After that, we started sp shopping in the gift shop, I bought a Sticky Splatter and a crystal. Once you had bought something, you could play on the play ground, it was extremely fun.

Next, they took us for a tour around the green house, the first animal we saw was the Chameleon, I was flabbergasted by the reason they camouflage, it was because they camouflage to show their feelings! The next animal we saw was the Dart frog, they were definetly my favourite out of all the ones I've saw. They were really bright, but not wild, so they were not poisonous.

After, my favourite, tour in the world, we all had lunch, outside, luckily after lunch we could go back over to the on play ground to play, I played on the huge swingset! Next, we quickly sprinted back to the green house do to do a special activity It was sketching all of the plants and animals. M

My favourite animal to sketch was the Anaconda, and my favourite plant, was the Dumb Cane.

Your's sincerely

James

Leo

Thursday 16th January 2014

Obj: To write a diary entry.

Day 1 (In the walls)

AARRRGGH! All I want to do is scream. Being trapped in these walls is agony; no gun, no games, no food and to talking what so ever. Basically, we saunter the through the downstairs, up the middle and into ajoining walls and all the time we have to be quieter than any mouse. The thing is my dad, the pack leader, is adamant that one of these humdrum days we will break through the walls walls of this house; furthermore we will drive away anyone who should dare to come within four inches of the house. I hate it here, consequently I am always in a *bad mood. If I tell you how how depressing it is in here then you will probably want to curl up in a miniscule ball on the floor! You'll probably think I am am bonkers but sometimes I feel as if the walls have ears or the walls track my every move like deers observing the wilderness around them. Anyway Anyway, I am enclosed in these walls, moreover there is nothing I can do - or is there?

In the walls with me are; My father, Bernard the pack leader, my mother, Dazzle, my grandfather, Timber and my big brother, Thunder. My grandfather is getting on a bit - he thinks we're in a cave, back in Canada, unfortunately no one has the heart to tell him we're not so it looks as though its going to stay that way until we make our move. I sicerely hope we make our move soon.

Day 2 (In the house)

We did it! Well Grandad did it - we were crouched in the wall the mother of tog s bedroom, when Grandad dozed off, he's quite a large and father

wolf so as he lent back he went crashing into the
Mother and Father's bedroom - it was hilarious! It was hilarious
until dad yelled, "Attack!" He said that he had devised a
cunning plan for us to follow. That was when my stomach
flipped, all of a sudden I felt guilty, it washed over me
without warning like a wave. It hit me that this family
was so innocent, as a result of this I had a word with
my dad (it didn't go too well). "What piffle!" He exclaimed.
"How silly dear," said my mother. Feeling sorry for myself, I
slumped back into the wall listening as my family
bashed and crashed in the kitchen.

Later that evening, I plucked up some much needed
courage and ventured downstairs to join in the party
games; jam throwing, stick the on
the jam jar, pass the jam on toast and many, many more.
Usually, I would have enjoyed it but the jam jars frowned
at me and the T.V. looked down on me in disgust. To
make matters worse the agonizing feeling of guilt followed
me everywhere like a swarm of fierce bees. Why can't we
just go home?

Emily

Bridge street
Woodville
HP94 9XJ

Dear Amelia,

Hi, are you alright? I haven't heard from you in a while. Anyway, I just had to tell ya about the most phenomenal experience that my class got last week when we visited the studio skills academy. Because it was so brilliant, I thought no school should miss out this exeptional oppotunity and that includes you. However, if you do go on the trip, it requires a lot of preparation in advance, so I suggest you scrutinize the following.

Beforehand you need to:

• Sort yourselves into teams.
• Then designate the different roles.

To help you and your teacher decide who will be suited to what role here is a list of them.

presenter - they are one of the few people on the screen. they work with the camera operator and introduce the report.

Director - the director works closely with the camera operator to make sure all the shots are perfect.

Producer - The producers role in the team is to make sure everything is running smoothly and on time.

Script writer - They need to be quite creative because their job is write a suitable script for the witnesses and presenter.

editor - their part in the group is to help the script writer and cut out all the bad parts from the report.

Camera operator - their role is to shoot the report and take advice from the director.

eyewitness - The witnesses job is to tell everybody what they have experienced.

expert - Their role is to give their opinion about what has happened and tell them all about what they know.

I really hope you are able to persuade your teacher to take you because she will really regret it is she says no.

Good luck

Emily xxx

Big Writing and the Oxford Writing Criterion Scale

Big Writing is an approach to teaching and assessing writing 'voice' within relevant contexts that grew out of the development of the Writing Criterion Scale. Developed by Ros Wilson, it is used in thousands of schools across the UK and worldwide and its enduring popularity and success can be put down to one thing: it works!

> *'Most teachers report that Big Writing has impacted positively on the whole school, identifying a range of benefits on the profile of writing [and] the quality of writing teaching and learning...'*

Initial Evaluation of the Impact of Big Writing, NFER, March 2014

When the *Big Writing* method is embraced and delivered well by staff across a whole-school, it has a positive impact on:

- Teacher subject knowledge and confidence to teach and assess writing effectively.
- Pupils' understanding of the writing process and what it means to be a 'good writer'.
- Pupils' confidence and enjoyment of writing.
- Writing standards – regardless of the circumstances of the school.

'If a child can't say it, a child can't write it.'

Big Writing is rooted in the belief that children can only write using the language they 'own' in their heads and that such language is acquired and refined most effectively through talk (which is an active cognitive process) rather than through reading and textual analysis.

The *Big Writing* methodology is therefore one in which pupils develop the ideas, vocabulary and higher level grammatical structures needed to improve their writing almost entirely through talk and oral rehearsal.

The Writer's Toolkit

To be a successful, high level writer an individual usually needs to be able to operate a number of skills simultaneously. In *Big Writing* this is called the Writer's Toolkit and is simplified into:

WHAT 1: the text type or genre
WHAT 2: the stimulus, or purpose and audience
HOW 1: basic skills – grammar, handwriting, spelling andpunctuation (GHaSP)
HOW 2: 'Writing Voice' or higher level language structures

WHAT to write: Text type and stimulus

Teachers are very capable and confident in the teaching of text types and in using a range of different stimuli for writing, and the 2014 National Curriculum in England places significant emphasis on children being able to write 'for a range of purposes and audiences'.

HOW to write 1: Basic skills

Most schools will have a structured approach to teaching basic skills, particularly spelling and handwriting, in Key Stage 1 and early Key Stage 2. In *Big Writing* it is recommended that 10 minutes a day of basic skills is continued right through to the end of Key Stage 2 so that no child is left behind. It is also important that 'best writing' in terms of basic skills is expected whenever children write.

HOW to write 2: Writing Voice

Big Writing is unique in focusing primarily on the development of 'Writing Voice' – that is, the higher level language structures that are specific to written language and which can be very different from spoken language. Writing Voice includes aspects of vocabulary, grammar and punctuation that are known in *Big Writing* as VCOP:

- **Vocabulary** – also known as WOW Words – that is ambitious and interesting.
- **Connectives** – expanding the range of linking, connecting and sequencing words including conjunctions, adverbs and prepositions.
- **Openers** – using a range of structures to open sentences, focusing on three 'power openers' as follows: -ly words (fronted adverbials), -ing words (participles) and connectives.
- **Punctuation** – teaching the full range of punctuation, including the use of power punctuation (? ! ...) for effect.

VCOP skills are taught through a series of fast, lively and predominantly oral activities that help to embed learning and make it fun. Children are explicitly taught that by improving their VCOP skills and their basic skills they can raise the standard of their writing.

The Big Write

The weekly Big Write session has become a popular feature of many schools. From Year 2 onwards the Big Write consists of two 45-minute sessions separated by play time.

The structure of the Big Write is as follows:

The evening before the Big Write:
- Set a 'Talk Homework' related to the text type or the topic children are going to write about.

Big Write Day, Session 1:
- 35 minutes of fast, fun, lively VCOP activities to build on existing skills and to respond to pupils' needs in light of writing assessments.
- 10 minutes of planning time – oral or diagrammatic rehearsal of writing.

Big Write Day, Session 2:
- 45 minutes of silent, individual writing.

After the Big Write:
- Mark and return children's writing promptly, focusing on VCOP and on performance against their individual writing targets.
- Allow 10–15 minutes for children to discuss their marked writing with a partner.

Visit www.andrelleducation.co.uk to find more detailed information about the *Big Writing* approach and training options, or consult the *Big Writing* books, published by Oxford University Press.

The Oxford Writing Criterion Scale and Oxford Programmes

Oxford University Press (OUP) and Andrell Education Ltd provide a number of programmes and resources that connect to the OWCS which can be used to develop children's talk and writing for a range of purposes as well as their basic skills. They support the effective implementation of the writing assessment and teaching cycle to ensure that progress actually happens!

The Writing Assessment and Teaching Cycle

1 Assess
Using the Oxford Writing Criterion Scale across the whole school for consistency

4 Track progress
Termly assessment supports progress tracking against expectations

Oxford Primary Writing Assessment

2 Identify
What can children can do in relation to expectations? What are their next steps?

3 Teach
Plan teaching around children's needs and next steps

Effective teaching and learning resources

1. *Big Writing*

The *Big Writing* method has been proven over many years to be a highly effective approach to raising standards in writing. The progress evidence from Cravenwood Academy, Manchester (see page xx) is just one example of the impact that is possible. The *Big Writing* training and resources have recently been updated to reflect the 2014 National Curriculum and, in particular, the higher grammar requirements. Training also includes use of the new Oxford Writing Criterion Scale.

For information about *Big Writing* and the CPD provided by Ros Wilson and her team, please visit www.andrelleducation.com or call the team at Andrell on 01924 229380

2. *Big Writing Adventures*

Big Writing Adventures is an exciting new online resource that combines rigorous skills progression with engaging stimulus materials to give children a real purpose and audience for writing.

Based around the *Big Writing* method and with progression directly linked to the Oxford Writing Criterion Scale, *Big Writing Adventures* is the best way of connecting assessment outcomes with high quality teaching and fun writing experiences for children.

3. *Nelson Grammar* and *Nelson Spelling*

These simple, easy-to-use resources have a clear structure and progression and can be used for focused skills work at any time.

The recent new editions are fully in line with the 2014 National Curriculum and include Revision Books and sample Grammar, Punctuation and Spelling Tests to help prepare children for the end of Key Stage tests from 2016.

Nelson Grammar   Nelson Spelling

4. *Nelson Handwriting*

The definitive handwriting programme – used in thousands of UK primary schools – continues to provide a clear framework for the teaching of handwriting across a whole school and is fully in line with the requirements of the 2014 National Curriculum.

If you would like information about any of the Oxford resources please visit: www.oxfordprimary.co.uk or call your local OUP education consultant.

Nelson Handwriting

On our Oxford Owl for schools website you will find:

- All the tracking and reporting sheets from this Handbook available to edit, print and download (find in: Teaching and Assessment Resources)
- A wealth of advice, expert videos and case studies about assessment (find in: PD and Best Practice)
- Two detailed school improvement 'pathways' for assessment (find in: Pathways)

Visit **www.oxford.owl.co.uk** to find out more.

The Expanded Oxford Writing Criterion Scale

Introduction

The following pages reproduce the Oxford Writing Criterion Scale found on pages 19–33 but with expanded descriptions for all criteria. Written by Ros Wilson, these expanded descriptions offer supplementary detail and additional examples of the evidence that teachers might expect to see for a particular skill.

The expanded OWCS is designed to guide and support all teachers, regardless of their experience of assessment, in making secure, confident judgements about every piece of writing that they assess.

Pre-Writing Standard: Early Years

PRE-WRITING STANDARD: Early Years

Name: Date:

No	Criteria	Expanded Description	Evidence? (✔, ✗, ●)
1	Will tolerate hand manipulation.	Allows the teacher to 'cover' their hand and 'guide' it in mark-making or drawing.	
2	Will work with another to allow mark-making using body parts or an implement.	Co-operates with another in the mark-making process, or even 'helps'. May be making positive and encouraging statements.	
3	Will attempt to mark-make independently.	Grasps mark-making tools or uses their finger (in paint, wet sand or similar) to make their first marks. The marks may be very small and faint initially, or very large and crude.	
4	Can recognize mark-making materials.	Shows through speech or behaviour (e.g. trying to hold/use a tool to make marks) that they know a tool is used in mark-making.	
5	Can use and enjoys mark-making materials.	Sometimes chooses to mark-make with little or no prompting. Their facial expression and/or body language indicate that they are enjoying mark-making.	
6	Can show some control in mark-making.	Moves from making random marks (which may be very small and faint or large and crude) to some evidence of controlled dragging or pushing of a line in a chosen direction.	
7	Can produce some recognizable letters.	Definite letter shapes are detectable (they may be embedded within and amongst other random mark-making) although they may still be very crude or irregular in size and form.	
8	Can differentiate between different letters and symbols.	When given a random assortment of shapes, either solid or written, the child can point correctly to most or all that are letters.	
9	Shows some awareness of the sequencing of letters.	Is obviously trying to order letters and to use the left to right formation to form a 'word' or some writing. (May use magnetic letters, card or wooden letters or their own mark-making.)	
10	Can copy over/under a model.	When given a few words or a line of writing, the child can copy it on the line above or below, usually fairly accurately.	
11	Can imitate adults' writing and understands the purpose of writing.	May do writing 'patterns' that resemble joined writing or print, but no actual letters are identifiable. May seek writing materials to achieve a purpose, e.g. in role-play as a doctor to write a prescription. May pretend to write with no mark-making tools. May ask someone else to do the writing during role-play.	
12	Can name three or more different purposes of writing.	Should be able to name at least three purposes, e.g. lists, labels, stories, poems, letters, shopping lists, etc.	
13	Can ascribe meaning to own mark-making ('reads' what has been 'written').	When asked, 'What have you written?' the child should attempt to 'read back' their 'writing', although they may be making it up as they go along.	
14	Knows print has meaning and that, in English, it is read from left to right and top to bottom.	May be pretending to 'read' a book or other text. The child can use their 'pointing finger' to follow the sequence of the text loosely as he/she reads, or follows the text with their eyes or head.	
15	Can write the initial letter of their own name.	They should always be able to produce a strong semblance to the initial letter of their own name, either in upper or lower case.	
16	Can attempt to 'write' things, including their own name, using random letters.	May only be a collection of letters or an occasional recognizable word in a jumble of letters, but the child usually states that it is 'writing' or it has been produced in response to being asked to write.	
17	Can write their own name, although it may be with wrong letter formations or mixed lower/upper case.	The name is almost always recognizable, although some letters may be reversed/inversed (b/d, g/p/q etc.) Capitals may be in the wrong places or not used at all, descenders or 'tails' may be above the line, etc.	
18	Can recognize their own first name when it is written in clear print.	Can pick out their own peg, book, book bag, etc. by reading their name on it.	

Standard 1: Reception/P1

STANDARD 1: Reception/P1

Name: Date:

No	Criteria	Expanded Description	Evidence? (✔, ✗, ●)
1	Can draw recognizable letters of the alphabet.	Every letter is recognizable, although size and shape may still be erratic.	
2	Can write their own name.	Can write their own first name with mainly appropriate upper/lower case letters, although size and shape may not be fully controlled.	
3	Can 'write' things using a mix of appropriate and random letters.	Can write simple labels, captions, etc. copying off the wall or in play (e.g. shopping lists) with a mix of correct and random letters. Some are decodable.	
4	Can sequence most of the letters of the alphabet.	Can write most of the alphabet or arrange wood, plastic, magnetic or similar letters in alphabetical order, with just a few mistakes.	
5	Can write their own name with the correct letter formations, although the size and shape may be slightly inconsistent.	Can write their own name with every letter shaped correctly, although size may still be variable and not always well-shaped.	
6	Can name the purpose of different texts/types of writing (at least three).	Can say when or why you might want to write at least three different types of text or can say what type of writing something is when they are shown it.	
7	Can 'read' what he/she has 'written'.	Can 'read back' a piece of writing they have done, although it may be from memory.	
8	Can hold and use a pencil effectively.	May not yet be the standard pencil grip, but they are able to control the pencil well enough to shape many letters correctly.	
9	Can spell some of the words from the Year R High Frequency Word list.	Can spell around half or more of the words on the Year R High Frequency word list.	
10	Can spell CVC (consonant, vowel, consonant) words (e.g. sit, bag, cat) usually correctly.	Can spell most CVC words correctly.	
11	Can write simple labels and captions.	Can make labels or captions for things in the classroom, using simple phonics to spell literally, e.g. pensil, trane, howse, briks.	
12	Can usually leave a space between emerging words.	Most words in writing are separated by finger spaces.	
13	Can show some control over word order, producing short logical statements, trying to use emergent phonics for spellings not known.	Can write short statements that can be read, with words usually in the correct order, e.g. 'I can run.' 'I play howse'.	
14	Can produce two or more logical statements on the same subject.	E.g. 'I play in howse.' 'I clene the floor.' The full stop may not be there or not in the correct place, but they can clearly write two or more statements.	
15	Can spell many words on the Year R High Frequency Word list.	There should not be more than 10 errors in spelling the words on the Year R High Frequency Word list.	
16	Is beginning to attempt to write simple known stories.	Can manage a simple retelling of a traditional tale, e.g. 'Goldiloks went to 3 bear howse. She ate food. She went bed.'	
17	Can say what they want to write, speaking in clearly defined statements or sentences.	Can tell an adult what they are going to write, speaking in identifiable sentences, i.e. with a pause between statements.	
18	Can spell many common, single syllable words correctly in writing, including most of the words in the Year R High Frequency Word list and the Early Years Outcomes.	There should not be more than six errors in spelling the words on the Year R High Frequency Word.	
19	Can write three or more simple statements on a given subject that can be read without the child's help and that make sense, although letter shapes and spelling may not be fully accurate.	Can make up and write three simple sentences on a subject given by the teacher, but with no other help. Handwriting, spelling, grammar and punctuation may not be fully accurate, but the writing can mainly be decoded without help.	
Total	0–2 = not yet working at this Standard; review against the Pre-Writing Standard. **3–8 ticks = Developing** **9–16 ticks = Secure** **17–19 ticks = Advanced** Assessment point: children with 18 or more ticks may be assessed against Standard 2.		

Standard 2: Year 1/P2

STANDARD 2: Year 1/P2

Name: Date:

No	Criteria	Expanded Description	Evidence? (✔, ✗, ●)
1	Can write their own first name with appropriate upper and lower case letters (may not be totally accurate).	The initial letter should be a capital and all the others lower case. Size and shape may not be fully accurate.	
2	Can form all letters clearly, although size and shape may be irregular.	Can write every letter of the alphabet clearly and legibly, although there may still be some irregularity in size and shape.	
3	Writes simple regular words, some spelt correctly.	Can spell all the words on the Year R High Frequency Word list and about half of the Year 1 High Frequency Word list and National Curriculum list.	
4	Almost always leaves spaces between words.	Every word has a clear space between it and the preceding/following words.	
5	Makes sensible phonic attempts at words.	All except complex words have logical spelling/use of phonics or known word rules and all words can be decoded.	
6	Can spell all CVC (consonant, vowel, consonant) words (e.g. sit, bag, cat) correctly.	There should be no errors in CVC words.	
7	Confidently writes some captions and labels and attempts other simple forms of writing (e.g. lists, stories, retellings etc.).	Can write simple and familiar labels and texts confidently, without support.	
8	Can show some control over letter size, shape and orientation in writing.	Writing is becoming even and controlled in size and shape.	
9	Can say what their writing says and means.	Can always 'read back' their writing.	
10	Can retell known stories in writing.	Can produce a short retelling of a familiar, known story, e.g. 'Goldiloks went to 3 bear howse. She ate food. She went bed.'	
11	Can produce their own ideas for writing (not a retelling)	Can make up simple stories and other texts.	
12	Can show some control over word order, producing logical statements.		
13	Can spell most of the Year R and 1 High Frequency Words and the Year 1 words in the N. C. Appendix 1.	Can spell all the words on the Year R and most of the words on the Year 1 High Frequency Word lists, with no more than 10 errors in total.	
14	Can make recognizable attempts at spelling words not known (almost all decodable without the child's help). (If all are spelt correctly, tick this criterion so as not to penalize the child).	In simple pieces of unsupported writing all, except a few ambitious words, are decodable and there are usually no more than three spelling errors (at the teacher's discretion: if the writing is above expectation there may be more errors).	
15	Can write simple texts such as lists, stories, reports, recounts (of a paragraph or more).	When asked to write a familiar type of text, they almost always write a sensible paragraph or more.	
16	Begins to show awareness of how full stops are used in writing. (May be in the wrong places or only one, final full stop.)	Always uses at least a final full stop in a piece of writing OR random full stops within the piece. If full stops are used correctly throughout, tick this criterion anyway.	
17	Can usually give letters a clear and regular size, shape and orientation (ascenders and descenders and use of upper and lower case are usually accurate).	Handwriting is becoming neat and regular with all tails below the line and all ascenders clearly above the lower case letters. All letters should face the correct way.	
18	Can use a connective (may only ever be 'and') to join two simple sentences, thoughts, ideas, etc.	Two or more items, statements or sentences in a paragraph of writing are extended, at a minimum through the use of 'and' or another simple conjunction (e.g. but, so, then).	
19	Can use appropriate vocabulary (should be coherent and sensible) in more than three statements.	Can always choose appropriate words/language for the type and purpose of a text.	

STANDARD 2: Year 1/P2 (cont.)

Name: Date:

No	Criteria	Expanded Description	Evidence? (✔, ✗, ●)
20	Can always use logical phonic strategies when trying to spell unknown words in more than three statements.	Even ambitious words have logical use of phonics and all can be decoded.	
21	Can usually use a capital letter and full stop, question mark or exclamation mark to punctuate sentences.	Most sentences are clearly punctuated with a capital letter at the start and a final piece of punctuation (which may only be a full stop).	
22	Can produce a paragraph or more of developed ideas independently that can be read without help from the child (may be more like spoken than written language but must not be a retelling).	Can always produce a sensible and appropriate paragraph or more of independent writing that can be fully decoded and makes sense. Basic Skills may not be fully accurate.	
Total	0–6 ticks = not yet working at this Standard; review against Standard 1. **7–12 ticks = Developing** **13–17 ticks = Secure** **18–22 ticks = Advanced** Assessment point: children with 20 or more ticks should be assessed against Standard 3.		

Standard 3: Year 2/P3

STANDARD 3: Year 2/P3

Name: Date:

No	Criteria	Expanded Description	Evidence? (✔, ✗, ●)
1	Can communicate ideas and meaning confidently in a series of sentences of at least a paragraph in length. (May not be accurate, but mainly 'flows' as it has lost the 'list like' form typical of some early writing.)	Can always produce a sensible and appropriate paragraph or more of independent writing that can be fully decoded and that makes sense. Some sentences should open in different ways.	
2	Can control use of ascenders/descenders and upper/lower case letters in handwriting.	Writing is neat and accurate.	
3	Can write in three or more text forms with reasonable accuracy. (If the writing is a narrative, simple report or recount of a known story this cannot be ticked. If it is another genre, it can be ticked as they will already know these three text forms).	This can only be assessed against a single piece of writing if the text type is other than a narrative, a known story recount or a simple report, as these are the first forms most children learn and if they have written one of these it cannot be assumed that they know any others. If they have written a more challenging text (e.g. an explanation, journalistic report, letter, etc.) it can be assumed that all three early forms are secure.	
4	Can provide enough detail to interest the reader (e.g. is beginning to provide additional information or description beyond a simple list).	May use simple description or provide additional information that was not essential to communicate the main point, but adds interest, e.g. stops to describe something or provides a simple explanation.	
5	Can vary the structure of sentences to interest the reader (e.g. questions, direct speech or opening with a subordinate clause, etc.).	Can vary the standard sentence structure of subject, verb, object, e.g. The dog (subject) ate (verb) the biscuit (object).	
6	Can sometimes use interesting and ambitious words (they should be words not usually used by a child of that age, and not a technical word used in a taught context only, e.g. 'volcano' in geography or 'evaporate' in science).	'WOW' words are words that make you go 'WOW!' if a child of that age uses them. Thus it is the ONLY age related criterion. By age 11, it should be assumed these will be adult WOW words.	
7	Can usually sustain narrative and non-narrative forms (can write at length – close to a side of A4 at least – staying on task).	Can write ¾ or more of a side of A4 paper (not wide lined and not oversized) staying on matters relevant to the subject or context of the writing.	
8	Can match organization to purpose (e.g. showing awareness of the structure of a letter, openings and endings, the importance of the reader, organizational devices, beginnings of paragraphing, etc.).	At least two organizational features of a given text should be present, e.g. in a letter, the address and signature or 'Dear XXX' and sign off; in instructions, the ingredients and a list of actions; in a narrative, three or more paragraphs for opening, body and ending.	
9	Can usually maintain the use of basic sentence punctuation (full stops followed by capital letters) in a piece close to a side of A4 in length. (May be on a shorter piece or may not be accurate to achieve the 'Developing' category.)	50% or more of all sentences in a piece are correctly punctuated.	
10	Can spell most common words correctly and most of the Years R, 1 & 2 High Frequency Words, and the Year 1 & 2 words in the N.C. Appendix 1.		
11	Can use phonetically plausible strategies to spell or attempt to spell unknown polysyllabic words. (If all the spelling is correct in a long enough piece to provide secure evidence, tick this criterion.)	Even most ambitious 'WOW' words have a logical phonic spelling and once a strategy has been used it should be maintained (i.e. if they spell 'persute' once, they must use that spelling every time UNLESS they switch to the correct spelling).	
12	Can use connectives other than 'and' to join two or more simple sentences, thoughts, ideas, etc. (e.g. but, so, then, or, when, if, that, because).	Uses three or more different connectives in longer pieces of writing (close to a side of A4 at least).	
13	Can use a range of punctuation, mainly correctly, including at least three of the following: full stop and capital letter, exclamation mark, question mark, comma (at least in lists), apostrophe for simple contraction and for singular possession (at least), e.g. 'John's dog...', 'The cat's bowl...'.	All Year 2 children should be taught to use the full stop/capital letter, comma, question mark, exclamation mark and apostrophe for simple possession and contraction accurately and be expected to demonstrate three or more of these punctuation marks in their writing.	

STANDARD 3: Year 2/P3 (cont.)

Name: Date:

No	Criteria	Expanded Description	Evidence? (✔, ✗, ●)
14	Can make their writing lively and interesting (e.g. provides additional detail, consciously uses humour, varies sentence length or uses punctuation to create effect, etc.).	When read aloud by a competent reader, the piece should be lively and interesting. There should be a good mix of ways of starting sentences, a mix of simple and compound sentences with some detail and description, three or more different types of punctuation and three or more different connectives.	
15	Can link ideas and events, using strategies to create 'flow' (e.g. Last time, also, after, then, soon, at last, and another thing…).	Openings of sentences and sections or paragraphs sometimes refer backwards or forwards in time or place, e.g. 'Before…','After…''Soon…','Next…', 'Later…','On Sunday…''Under…''Beside…'.	
16	Can use adjectives and descriptive phrases for detail and emphasis (consciously selects the adjective for purpose, rather than using a familiar one, e.g. a title: 'Big Billy Goat Gruff').	ANY attempts at description may be counted here (as long as they are not known labels or names containing adjectives, e.g. Little Red Hen). There does not have to be a number of different types, although it is usually useful to see three or more examples (which may all be one type, e.g. adjectives).	
17	Structures basic sentences correctly, including capitals and full stops in a longer piece (one error is acceptable).	The writing should be 90% accurate when it is over one side of A4. (NB: If a child is using punctuation beyond normal expectations there may be more errors.)	
18	Can use accurate and consistent handwriting (in print at a minimum, can show consistent use of upper/lower case, ascenders/descenders, size and form).	Handwriting should always be neat and well formed. All ascenders should show clearly above the line of writing and all descenders should be clearly below. Capitals should always be used correctly.	
19	Begins to show evidence of joined handwriting.	Some words should be consciously and clearly joined.	
20	Uses past and present tenses correctly.	Uses the simple past and present tenses accurately and consistently.	
21	Can produce close to a side (or more) of A4 writing that is clear and coherent with one or more strong features.	Writes confidently at length with a few good examples of features described in criteria 5, 6, 12, 13, 15 and 16.	
Total	0–5 ticks = not yet working at this Standard; review against Standard 2 **6–9 ticks = Developing** **10–16 ticks = Secure** **17–21 ticks = Advanced** (KS1 Mastery) Assessment point: children with 18 or more ticks should be assessed against Standard 4.		

Standard 4: Year 3/P4

STANDARD 4: Year 3/P4

Name: Date:

No	Criteria	Expanded Description	Evidence? (✔, ✗, ●)
1	Can produce work which is organized, imaginative and clear (e.g. simple opening and ending).	In a longer piece (3/4 of a side of A4 or more) there is a clear sequence with a recognizable opening, body and ending. It is lively and coherent, staying on task.	
2	Can usually join their handwriting.		
3	Can use a range of chosen forms appropriately and consistently. (If the writing is a narrative, simple report or recount of a known story this cannot be ticked. If it is another genre, it can be ticked as they will already know these three text forms).	This can only be assessed against a single piece of writing if the text type is other than a narrative, a known story recount or a simple report, as these are the first forms most children learn and if they have written one of these it cannot be assumed that they know any others. If they have written a more challenging text (e.g. an explanation, journalistic report, letter, etc.) it can be assumed that all three early forms are secure.	
4	Can adapt their chosen form to the audience (e.g. provide information about characters or setting, make a series of points, use brackets for asides, etc.).	Some types of text are adaptations in their own right, e.g. letters, play scripts and instructions. In other types, examples might be: direct speech, brackets or other parenthesis, headings, side headings, bullets and lists, questions or direct appeal to the reader or change of font for emphasis or effect.	
5	Can sometimes use interesting and ambitious words (they should be words not usually used by a child of that age, and not a technical word used in a taught context only, e.g. 'volcano' in geography or 'evaporate' in science).	'WOW' words are words that make you go 'WOW!' if a child of that age uses them. Thus it is the ONLY age related criterion. By age 11, it should be assumed these will be adult WOW words.	
6	Can develop and extend ideas logically in sequenced sentences (but they may still be overly detailed or brief).	There should be more than one sentence (usually on an on important point) that amplifies it or provides additional information. Additional information may be within sentences, through the use of brackets or similar. There will be clear logic to the way sentences develop.	
7	Can extend sentences using a wider range of connectives to clarify relationships between points and ideas (e.g. when, because, if, after, while, also, as well).	The writer may still be using the range of connectives from Year 2 (but, so, then, or, when, if, that, because) but should also be using more challenging ones, e.g. while, as, after, also, as well as, although, however.	
8	Can usually use correct grammatical structures in sentences (nouns and verbs generally agree).	In a longer piece, there should not be more than two grammatical errors.	
9	Can use pronouns appropriately to avoid the awkward repetition of nouns.	After using the noun, a pronoun is used to refer back to something a second or third time. E.g. 'he', 'she', 'it', 'they', 'we', etc.	
10	Can use most punctuation accurately, including at least three of the following: full stop and capital letter, question mark, exclamation mark, comma, apostrophe.	All sentences should have the correct use of the opening capital and the final piece of punctuation. There should be a wider range of punctuation used and they may be starting to use forms of parenthesis (brackets, double comma, double dash).	
11	Can structure and organize work clearly (e.g. beginning, middle, end; letter structure; dialogue structure).	Can use the features of the required type of text (which must have been previously taught and embedded) with 90% accuracy.	
12	Is beginning to use paragraphs.	There may only be one division, giving two large paragraphs, or there may be a series of very short paragraphs. They may or may not follow normal conventions (e.g. leaving a line between paragraphs and/or indenting.)	
13	Can adapt form and style for purpose (e.g. there is a clear difference between formal and informal letters; use of abbreviated sentences in notes and diaries, etc.).	Shows evidence of a change of 'voice' for characterization, e.g. in dialogue between different types of characters, in a formal tone for impersonal letters, in a chatty style for informal letters or diary entries.	
14	Can write neatly, legibly and accurately, mainly in a joined style.	Handwriting is now almost all joined, although this may lead to a temporary loss of neatness which should not be penalized.	

STANDARD 4: Year 3/P4 (cont.)

Name: Date:

No	Criteria	Expanded Description	Evidence? (✔, ✗, ●)
15	Can use adjectives and adverbs for description.	It is useful to see three good examples, but this rule must not be applied rigidly. Two exceptional examples are often enough. Low level examples that are learnt by all children cannot be counted as they are known as labels and the child may still not know it is good to describe. E.g. 'good girl', 'nice day', 'bad hair day', 'long jump'.	
16	Can spell phonetically regular, or familiar common polysyllabic words accurately (sometimes for the 'Developing' category) and most or all of the Year 3 High Frequency Words and the Year 3 words in the N.C. Appendix 1.	All CVC words and words from the Years R, 1 and 2 NC and High Frequency Word lists should now be accurate, as should all regular two and three syllable words that follow spelling rules or are made up of composite simple words or words with common prefixes/suffixes, e.g. 'Bonfire', 'sometimes', 'longing', 'parsnip', 'ransack', 'unhelpful', etc. 50% or more of the Year 3 High Frequency Word List and words from the NC Appendix 1 should be accurate.	
17	Can develop characters and describe settings, feelings and/or emotions, etc.	This takes more than one sentence and should include additional information beyond that needed for the theme to be coherent. It may be built into the text, e.g. 'John entered the room. He was struggling to carry a very large bag that seemed to be stuffed with something.' Alternatively, it can be in direct asides or comments to the reader, e.g. 'Lions live in Africa (although some lions do live in captivity in other countries) and usually live in packs called 'prides'.	
18	Can link and relate events, including past, present and future, sensibly (afterwards, before, also, after a while, eventually, etc.	Will confidently use a wide range of time, sequence and cause links, including those from Year 2, e.g. 'Before…', 'After…', 'Soon…', 'Next…', 'After a while…', 'Before very long…', etc. These may be either at the beginning or within sentences.	
19	Can attempt to give opinion, interest or humour through detail.	One good example is enough, although there may be more. Achieving criterion 17 would indicate an opinion, additional interest or an intention to be humorous. E.g. 'John entered the room slowly. In fact, if he had been going much slower he would have stopped!' or 'Lions live in Africa (and that is where they should all stay!)'	
20	Can use generalizing words for style (e.g. sometimes, never, always, often, mainly, mostly, generally, etc.) and/or modal verbs/the conditional tense (e.g. might do it, may go, could rain, should win).	Generalizing words are used to qualify or determine the degree of frequency or quantity. The conditional tense (modal verbs) uses generalizers with a verb, e.g. must xxxx, might xxxx, may xxx, could xxx, etc.	
21	Is beginning to develop a sense of pace (writing is lively and interesting).	Pace can be created in many ways. The piece should flow and have no evidence of a list-like, repetitive form. It should be interesting, with a mix of longer, more complex sentences and shorter, 'punchier' ones. There should be evidence of a range of openers, some of which should be striking. There may also be managed use of punctuation for effect and impact, e.g. question marks, exclamation marks, etc.	
Total	0–5 ticks = not yet working at this Standard; review against Standard 3. **6–9 ticks = Developing** **10–17 ticks = Secure** **18–21 ticks = Advanced** Assessment point: children with 19 or more ticks should be assessed against Standard 5.		

Standard 5: Year 4/P5

STANDARD 5: Year 4/P5

Name: Date:

No	Criteria	Expanded Description	Evidence? (✔, ✗, ●)
1	Can write in a lively and coherent style.	Voice and style are well established, with good variations in sentence type, length and structure and vocabulary. Shows interest in the subject. These features are maintained and confident.	
2	Can use a range of styles and genres confidently and independently. (If the writing is a narrative, simple report or recount of a known story this cannot be ticked. If any other genre, it can be ticked as they will already know these three text forms.)	Besides the three basic types of text, the child should be able to write for persuasion, journalistic reports, explanation, texts with instructions embedded, discursive texts or letters for a variety of purposes. Style and voice should be adapted according to the purpose and/or text type, the audience and genre.	
3	Can sometimes use interesting and ambitious words (they should be words not usually used by a child of that age, and not a technical word used in a taught context only, e.g.' volcano' in geography or 'evaporate' in science).	'WOW' words are words that make you go 'WOW!' if a child of that age uses them. Thus this is the ONLY age related criterion. By age 11, it should be assumed these will be adult WOW words.	
4	Can organize ideas appropriately for both purpose and reader (e.g. captions, headings, bullets, fonts, chapters, letter formats, paragraphs, logically sequenced events, contextual and background information etc.).	Can use a good range of organizational devices within a range of texts, as appropriate, e.g. sub-headings, captions, fonts, chapters, paragraphs, accurate dialogue structure, letter format, lists, bullets, etc.	
5	Can use a wide range of punctuation mainly accurately, including at least three of the following: full stop and capital letter, question mark, exclamation mark, apostrophe and comma.	The writer uses a wide range of punctuation, almost always accurately (at least 80% correct).	
6	Can write neatly, legibly and accurately, usually maintaining a joined style.		
7	Can use more sophisticated connectives (e.g. although, however, nevertheless, despite, contrary to, as well as, etc.).	The writer will be using many of the connectives indicated in Standard 4 plus some more sophisticated ones.	
8	Can use links to show time and cause.	Uses some of the links identified in Standard 4, as well as more ambitious ones, e.g. 'After a while...', 'Before very long...', 'Sometime later...', 'Eventually...', 'Consequently...', 'As a result of...', 'In order to...', etc. These may be either at the beginning or within sentences.	
9	Can open sentences in a wide range of ways for interest and impact.	Sometimes opens sentences in more interesting ways, e.g. causal, time and sequence connectives, 'ly' words or 'ing' words.	
10	Can use paragraphs, although they may not always be accurate.	There should be at least two clear paragraphs. These may not yet always be at the most appropriate point in the text and may not have an indentation. There may be two lines left empty.	
11	Can produce thoughtful and considered writing (uses simple explanation, opinion, justification and deduction).	The writer intersperses asides, comments, brackets, explanations, detailed descriptions, opinions and/or justification when appropriate. One good example is sufficient.	
12	Can use or attempt grammatically complex structures (e.g. expansion before and after the noun: 'The little, old man who lived on the hill...', '... by the lady who taught me the guitar...'; subordinate clauses: 'I felt better when...', etc.).	The writer sometimes uses phrases to describe, rather than just single adjectives or adverbs, or is beginning to try to use strategies such as the "w' trick' ('who, with, when, where, what' in the middle of a sentence) to create clauses, connectives, 'ly' words and 'ing' words.	
13	Can spell unfamiliar regular polysyllabic words accurately and most or all of the Year 4 High Frequency Words and the Year 4 words in the N.C. Appendix 1.	The writer is now a confident and accurate speller and usually only makes mistakes in irregular, complex words, for example: psychic, sophisticated, anxious, dialogue, sphinx, rhyme, etc.	
14	Can use nouns, pronouns and tenses accurately and consistently throughout.	Grammar is almost always correct (at least 90% correct).	

STANDARD 5: Year 4/P5 (cont.)

Name: Date:

No	Criteria	Expanded Description	Evidence? (✔, ✗, ●)
15	Can use apostrophes and/or inverted commas, mainly accurately. (If direct speech is not appropriate to the task, apostrophes alone can score the tick).	The writer uses apostrophes both for possession and for omission, and speech marks to designate direct speech, almost always accurately (at least 80% correct).	
16	Can select from a range of known adventurous vocabulary for a purpose, with some words being particularly well chosen.	'WOW' words are words that make you go 'WOW!' if a child of that age uses them. Thus this is the ONLY age related criterion. By age 11, it should be assumed these will be adult WOW words. By Year 4 some truly sophisticated words should be appearing which may be used slightly inaccurately at first.	
17	Can select interesting strategies to move a piece of writing forward (e.g. asides, characterization, dialogue with the audience, dialogue , etc.).	Within a longer piece, the writer interweaves elements that show awareness of the needs of the reader or to increase interest and detail. E.g. '(He always does that)', 'You may find it hard to believe that…', 'If you do this, I will be sure to…'	
18	Can advise assertively, although not confrontationally, in factual writing (e.g. 'An important thing to think about before deciding…', 'We always need to think about…', etc.).	This may only be developing at Standard 5. It is commonly found in persuasion and discursive writing, but the writer may now be experimenting with it in other text forms. Examples are commonly also found in direct speech in narratives, e.g. "We really should get going, it is beginning to rain," urged Jack.	
19	Can develop ideas in creative and interesting ways.	Writing should be fully independent, original and creative, and therefore unique to the writer.	
Total	0–5 ticks = not yet working at this Standard; review against Standard 4. **6–9 ticks = Developing** **10–15 ticks = Secure** **16–19 ticks = Advanced** Assessment point: children with 17 or more ticks should be assessed against Standard 6.		

Oxford Primary Writing Assessment

Standard 6: Year 5/P6

No	Criteria	Expanded Description	Evidence? (✔, ✗, ●)
1	Can produce well-structured and organized writing using a range of conventions in layout.	Evidences two or more organizational features confidently and accurately, e.g. letter features, paragraphing, headings, sub-headings, lists, bullets, brackets, columns, etc. as appropriate to the text.	
2	Can use appropriate informal and formal styles with confidence (e.g. conversational, colloquial, dialect, Standard English).	Voice and style are well-established and show clear evidence of adaptation to the purpose and audience. When appropriate, the style may change within a text. There is good variation in sentence type, length and structure, and vocabulary. The writer shows empathy with the subject.	
3	Can select the correct genre for audience and purpose, and use it accurately.	Has a wide grasp of the main features of text types, including a range of reporting styles, explanation, instruction, persuasion and discussion. The type of text required for purpose is always used accurately, with a good range of appropriate features.	
4	Can select from a wide range of known imaginative and ambitious vocabulary (words that are not usually used by a child of that age) and use them precisely. (All spelling, including that of complex words, is almost always correct.)	The writer uses some highly sophisticated vocabulary and yet spelling is almost totally accurate (at least 95% correct).	
5	Can use paragraphs consistently and appropriately.	Paragraphing is used accurately to sub-divide longer texts.	
6	Can group things appropriately before or after a main verb (e.g. 'The books, the pens and the pencils were all ready on the table').	There should be a string of three or more nouns or verbs (some with expansion) before or after the main verb, e.g. 'The old man, the boy and the dog were walking on the beach.' OR 'My mother gave me a new purse, a shirt and three books for my birthday.' Some may be beginning to be more widely expanded, e.g. 'I love wandering in the lush meadows, paddling in the warm shallows and resting under a tall tree while listening to the rustle of its leaves.'	
7	Can use all grammar accurately except when consciously using dialect or colloquialism for purpose and audience.	There are no unintentional grammatical errors.	
8	Can use different techniques to open or conclude work appropriately (e.g. opinion, summary, justification, comment, suspense or prediction).	Openings or endings have obviously been created for impact or effect, when appropriate, to draw the reader in or to leave them wanting more.	
9	Can use complex sentence structures appropriately.	The writer uses sophisticated sentence structures that include clauses as openers, embedded clauses, expansion and parenthesis. They may be beginning to use the passive voice.	
10	Can use a wider range of punctuation, almost always accurately, to include three or more of the following (as appropriate to the text): comma, apostrophe, bullets, inverted commas, hyphen, brackets, colon or semi-colon.	The writer uses a wide range of punctuation, almost always accurately (around 95% correct).	
11	Can use punctuation appropriately to create effect (e.g. exclamation mark, dash, question mark, ellipsis).	The writer consciously uses punctuation to create effect (! ? … -)	
12	Can write neatly, legibly and accurately in a flowing, joined style.	Handwriting is neat, joined and easily read.	
13	Can adapt handwriting for a range of tasks and purposes, including for effect.	The writer uses capitalization, italics or, etc. writing when appropriate.	
14	Can spell accurately in all but the most complex words (e.g. paraphernalia, quintessential etc.) and most or all of the Year 5 High Frequency Words and the Year 5 words in the N.C. Appendix 1.	Spelling in writing that includes ambitious words is 95% accurate or better. The piece cannot be assessed against this criterion if no complex words are used.	

STANDARD 6: Year 5/P6

Name: Date:

STANDARD 6: Year 5/P6 (cont)

Name: Date:

No	Criteria	Expanded Description	Evidence? (✔, ✗, ●)
15	Can use the passive voice for variety and to shift focus (e.g. 'The cake was eaten by the child').	The passive voice eliminates the need to name the person (e.g. 'Cake is often enjoyed in the afternoon.') Or it uses the object of the sentence as the main focus for emphasis, e.g. 'Trains may be preferred by travellers, to speed up their journeys.'	
16	Can use a range of narrative techniques with confidence, interweaving elements when appropriate (e.g. action, dialogue, quotation, formal or informal style, aside, observation, suspense).	A wide range of features may be used confidently and appropriately. The expanded grouping in criterion 6 is further exemplification of this.	
17	Can vary sentence length and word order confidently to sustain interest (e.g. 'Having achieved your goals at such an early age, what motivates you to continue? Why fight on?').	This may sometimes be exemplified in direct speech, e.g. 'I was running swiftly down the golden beach when I stood on the concealed shard of glass. "OUCH!" I exclaimed.'	
18	Can use a range of devices to adapt writing to the needs of the reader (e.g. headings, sub-headings, bullets, underlining, parenthesis, introduction providing context, footnote, contents, bibliography).	The writer can use organizational devices confidently and flexibly for purpose. This can be well illustrated in hybrid texts, e.g. a newspaper report or a set of instructions within a narrative or a letter.	
19	Can use literary features to create effect (e.g. alliteration, onomatopoeia, figurative language, dialect, metaphor, simile etc.).	Examples include: the soft, springy surface (alliteration), the thump of the machine (onomatopoeia), spring dawned like a blushing bride (simile), the car leapt out of the thicket (metaphor), etc.	
20	Can interweave implicit and explicit links between sections.	The writer uses time and sequence links confidently to give the piece greater coherence and sometimes uses referrals, e.g. 'As was stated earlier...', 'Returning to...', 'As will soon be explained...', etc.	
21	Can use punctuation to show division between clauses, to indicate, to vary pace, to create atmosphere or to sub-divide (e.g. commas, colons, semicolons, dashes, ellipses).	All punctuation can be used accurately in more sophisticated sentence structures, when appropriate to the text.	
22	Can show confident and established 'voice'.	It may difficult to find any way the 'voice' or style might be improved, although there may still be one or two tiny technical errors.	
Total	0–7 ticks = not yet working at this Standard; review against Standard 5. **8–11 ticks = Developing** **12–18 ticks = Secure** **19–22 ticks = Advanced** Assessment point: children with 20 or more ticks should be assessed against Standard 7.		

Standard 7: Year 6/P7

STANDARD 7: Year 6/P7

Name: Date:

No	Criteria	Expanded Description	Evidence? (✔, ✗, ●)
1	Can spell all vocabulary correctly apart from rare technical or obscure words. (Must have used unusual, ambitious vocabulary that is spelt correctly.)	It is rare to see a spelling error and if there is one it will be in terminology such as 'crustacean', 'quintessential', 'pseudonym', etc.	
2	Can open and close writing in interesting, unusual or dramatic ways, when appropriate.	Uses quirks, cliff hangers, suspense, the unexpected, the dramatic, etc. to 'grab' the reader at the beginning or to leave the reader wanting more at the end, when appropriate.	
3	Can use the full range of punctuation accurately and precisely, including for sub-division, effect, listing, direct speech, parenthesis, etc.	Creates opportunities to showcase a wide range of punctuation, when appropriate. (There should be a maximum of two errors.)	
4	Can write neatly, legibly, accurately and fluently, in a joined style.	Handwriting is attractive and contributes to the appeal of the piece.	
5	Can vary font for effect or emphasis when appropriate (print, italics or capitalization). There may only be one example.	Decorative handwriting such as 'ghost' writing or 'spikey' writing are also examples.	
6	Can use a wide range of conventions appropriately to the context, e.g. paragraphs, sub and side headings, addendum, footnote, contents, etc.	Creates opportunities to demonstrate their ability to use appropriate conventions. If there are none evidenced this is because they were not appropriate for the piece.	
7	Can use a wide range of sophisticated connectives, including conjunctions, adverbs and prepositions, to show time, cause, sequence and mode, including to open sentences sometimes.	Uses a range of standard connectives, plus more subtle or sophisticated examples such as: although, however, despite, in spite of, additionally, consequently, subsequently, ultimately, as a result of, even though, previously, etc.	
8	Can use clauses confidently and appropriately for audience and purpose.	This includes the correct use of punctuation to clarify meaning and/or relationships between clauses.	
9	Can use implicit links within a text, e.g. referring back to a point made earlier or forward to more information or detail to come.	Links are often embedded within text and are many and various. E.g. 'I thought I had been there before, but…', 'We hadn't expected to see them here, however…', 'I had hoped we would be able to…', 'He always used to think that…', etc.	
10	Can use complex groupings for effect, before or after the verb. There may only be one example.	Creates opportunities for a complex grouping, when appropriate, e.g. 'How I love the warmth of the summer breeze, the lapping of the gentle waves and the soft swish of the sand beneath my sandals.'	
11	Can use a range of techniques to interact or show awareness of the audience, e.g. action, dialogue, quotation, aside, suspense, tension, comment.	Creates opportunities to demonstrate secure knowledge of different techniques for variety, impact or effect when appropriate. If none are demonstrated, could they have been?	
12	Can write with maturity, confidence and imagination.	The writing is similar to that of a literate adult, although the subject matter may still be more appropriate to the age or experience of the writer.	
13	Can adapt writing for the full range of purposes, always showing awareness of audience and purpose.	Creates opportunities to demonstrate the use of features and techniques, which may include the use of hybrid texts (see criterion 14) and goes beyond the obvious or standard examples.	
14	Can consciously vary levels of formality according to purpose and audience.	This may be through the different 'voices' of two or more characters, through the use of a hybrid text (a text within a text) or through the quotation of a different writer, etc.	
15	Can sustain a convincing viewpoint throughout the piece of writing, e.g. authoritative, expert, convincing portrayal of character, opposing opinions, etc.	This may often be through correct interpretation of the features of a particular text type and thus may duplicate an earlier criterion.	

STANDARD 7: Year 6/P7 (cont)

Name: Date:

No	Criteria	Expanded Description	Evidence? (✔, ✗, ●)
16	Can use a wide range of ambitious vocabulary accurately and precisely (they should be words that are not usually used by a child of that age).	Vocabulary choices sometimes surprise, or cause amazement, for a child of that age. See examples in criterion 1.	
17	Can use two or more stylistic features to create effect within the text, e.g. rhetorical questions, repetition, figurative language, passive voice, metaphor, simile, alliteration, onomatopoeia, groupings, elaboration, nominalization, impersonal voice or universal appeal.	Creates opportunities to showcase sophisticated skills whenever possible and appropriate. This is now well-managed and feels 'natural' to the style of the writer.	
18	Can use creative and varied sentence structures when appropriate, intermingling with simple structures for effect.	Creates opportunities to use a wide range of sentence structures and types for impact and effect. This is now well-managed and feels 'natural' to the style of the writer.	
19	Can always construct grammatically correct sentences, unless using dialect or alternative constructions consciously for effect.	There are no grammatical errors, unless intentional and suited to the purpose.	
20	Can use pertinent and precise detail as appropriate.	Creates natural-feeling opportunities for detail and description to enrich the text and add interest, when appropriate.	
21	Can demonstrate a wide range of the criteria in Standard 7 effectively and in a well-managed and mature way, within a single piece of totally independent writing (of at least one and a half sides of A4).	Has learned and can use the vast majority of the skills described in Standard 7, naturally and effectively. This will be in a correct response to a stimulus and purpose, and thus only enables the skills appropriate within the piece.	
Total	0–6 ticks = not yet working at this Standard; review against Standard 6. **7–10 ticks = Developing** **11–17 ticks = Secure** **18–21 ticks = Advanced**		

Appendix 2: Commentary on Un-assessed Writing Samples

The following assessor commentary and judgements apply to the exemplar writing on pages 78–89. They have been ordered by Standard, from Pre-Writing to Standard 7.

Billy   Pre-Writing Standard

No	Criteria	Evidence?	Notes
1	Will tolerate hand manipulation.	✔	Assume he is beyond this stage as he can write his own name.
2	Will work with another to allow mark-making using body parts or an implement.	✔	Assume he is beyond this stage as he can write his own name.
3	Will attempt to mark-make independently.	✔	His name shows he is beyond this stage.
4	Can recognize mark-making materials.	✔	Assume he is beyond this stage as he can write his own name.
5	Can use and enjoys mark-making materials.	✔	Wrote willingly/cheerfully.
6	Can show some control in mark-making.	✔	Control is shown through staying mainly between two lines and through writing his name.
7	Can produce some recognizable letters.	✔	This is demonstrated in his name.
8	Can differentiate between different letters and symbols.	–	Uncertain from this. Would need to provide a mix and ask him to pick out the letters.
9	Shows some awareness of sequencing of letters.	✔	This is shown through writing his name.
10	Can copy over/under a model.	–	Billy would need to be asked to do this to confirm.
11	Can imitate adults' writing and understands the purpose of writing.	✔	The line of mark-making shows this.
12	Can name three or more different purposes of writing.	–	Would need to do a 'classroom walk' with him to assess this, 'spotting' writing and saying what job it does.
13	Can ascribe meaning to own mark-making ('reads' what has been 'written').	✔	Billy's response has been scribed below: 'Spider Man and DVD'
14	Knows print has meaning and that, in English, it is read from left to right and top to bottom.	✔	There is a clear orientation in both the mark-making and in the writing of his name.
15	Can write the initial letter of their own name.	✔	All the letters are correct except for the size of the 'i'.
16	Can attempt to 'write' things, including their own name, using random letters.	✔	The mark-making, plus the ability to say what it means, is good evidence of this.
17	Can write their own name, although it may be with wrong letter formations or mixed lower/upper case.	✔	Billy's name is a good example of this.
18	Can recognize their own first name, when it is written clearly in print.	–	Would need to do a 'classroom walk' with him to see if he can pick out his own peg, book, book bag or similar.

Assessment score

Score = 14/14 (4 criteria not assessable so thresholds must be lowered by 4).

Jo Standard 1: Reception

No	Criteria	Evidence?	Notes
1	Can draw recognizable letters of the alphabet.	✔	Every letter is recognizable although size and shape are still be erratic.
2	Can write their own name.	✔	'Jo' is correct, although it is a simple name.
3	Can 'write' things using a mix of appropriate and random letters.	✔	Writing is fully decodable.
4	Can sequence most of the letters of the alphabet.	✔	This writing could not have been done without the sequencing of letters in the alphabet being secure.
5	Can write their own name with correct letter formation, although size and shape may still be slightly inconsistent.	✔	'Jo' is correct.
6	Can name the purpose of different texts/types of writing (at least three).	✔	This is a retell – one of the early forms of writing. Jo should be able to write captions, labels and simple reports (news) so should be able to name them.
7	Can 'read' what he/she has 'written'.	✔	Can assume so by this stage, but should confirm by asking her to 'read' her writing.
8	Can hold and use a pencil effectively.	✔	Jo is able to control the pencil well enough to shape and orientate letters correctly.
9	Can spell some of the words from the Year R High Frequency Word list.	–	9 words out of 16, plus her name, are correct – roughly half, but should assess separately.
10	Can spell CVC (consonant, vowel, consonant) words (e.g. sit, bag, cat) usually correctly.	–	'to', 'up', 'and', 'went', 'into', 'food' are loosely VC or CV or CVC, but could all be sight words, so there is not enough evidence to judge – should assess separately.
11	Can write simple labels and captions.	✔	Jo's writing is beyond this stage.
12	Can usually leave a space between emerging words.	✔	All correct.
13	Can show some control over word order producing short logical statements, trying to use emergent phonics for spellings not known.	✔	All words are decodable and all statements logical except for the 'A castle' out of sequence.
14	Can produce two or more logical statements on the same subject.	✔	There are three statements.
15	Can spell many words on the Year R High Frequency Word List.		Need to assess this separately.
16	Is beginning to attempt to write simple known stories.	✔	This is clearly based on a retell of 'Jack and the Beanstalk.'
17	Can say what they want to write, speaking in clearly defined statements or sentences.	–	Not assessable.
18	Can spell many common, single syllable words correctly in writing, including most of the words in the Year R High Frequency Word list and the Early Years Outcomes.	✗	Spelling here suggests it is weak generally. Should assess separately.
19	Can write three or more simple statements on a given subject that can be read without the child's help and that make sense, although letter shapes and spelling may not be fully accurate.	✔	There are three statements, all of which make sense: 'I climbed up the beanstalk. / and I went into a castle / then I saw some food' The random 'A castle' is not counted as there are still three clear statements.

Assessment score

0–2 ticks = not yet working at this Standard; review against Pre-Writing Standard.
3–8 ticks = Developing
9–16 ticks = Secure
17–19 ticks = Advanced
Assessment point: children with 18 or more ticks may be assessed against Standard 2.

Score = 14/15 (4 criteria not assessable so thresholds must be lowered by 4).
Judgement = Standard 1A. May go on to assess for Standard 2.

Oxford Primary Writing Assessment

Usman   Standard 2: Year 1

No	Criteria	Evidence?	Notes
1	Can write their own first name with appropriate upper and lower case letters (may not be totally accurate).	✔	'Usman'
2	Can form all letters clearly, although size and shape may be irregular.	✔	All letters are the correct shape, although size, capital/small and ascender/descenders are still erratic.
3	Writes simple regular words, some spelt correctly.	✔	Many words are correct.
4	Almost always leaves spaces between words.	✔	Every word has a clear space between it and the preceding/following words except at end of lines.
5	Makes sensible phonic attempts at words.	✔	All words are decodable and logical in terms of phonics except two: 'favroit' for 'favourite' and 'exsersed' for 'exhausted'. This may be connected to the way he speaks.
6	Can spell all CVC (consonant, vowel, consonant) words correctly.	✔	E.g. 'am', 'to', 'well', 'now', 'can', 'up', 'bit', 'did'.
7	Confidently writes some captions and labels and attempts other simple forms of writing (e.g. lists, stories, retell etc.).	✔	The writing shows that he is well beyond this stage.
8	Can show some control over letter size, shape and orientation in writing.	●	Letter size, capital/small, ascender/descenders all need work.
9	Can say what their writing says and means.	✔	The writing is beyond this stage.
10	Can retell known stories in writing.	✔	The writing is well beyond this stage as it is a letter of congratulations with historical connections.
11	Can produce their own ideas for writing (not a retelling).	✔	This was a given task with some true references from history, but the content is his own composition.
12	Can show some control over word order, producing logical statements.	✔	The writing is a good paragraph of logical statements.
13	Can spell most of the Year R and 1 High Frequency words and the Year 1 words in the N.C. Appendix 1.	–	This needs to be assessed separately.
14	Can make recognizable attempts at spelling words not known, (almost all decodable without the child's help). (If all are spelt correctly, tick this criterion so as not to penalize the child for being a good speller).	✔	All words are decodable except, perhaps, 'exsersed' (exhausted).
15	Can write simple texts such as lists, stories, reports, recounts (of a paragraph or more).	✔	This is a good length paragraph, even if the handwriting was a more appropriate size.
16	Begins to show awareness of how full stops are used in writing. (May be in the wrong places or only one, final full stop.)	✔	All full stops are correctly placed, but often not followed by capitals.
17	Can usually give letters a clear and regular size, shape and orientation (ascenders/descenders and use of upper/lower case are usually accurate).	✗	Letters are not accurate.
18	Can use ANY connective (may only ever be 'and') to join two simple sentences, thoughts, ideas, etc.	✔	E.g. 'with', 'and', 'also'.
19	Can use appropriate vocabulary (should be coherent and sensible) in their writing.	✔	Vocabulary used is coherent and sensible.
20	Can always use logical phonic strategies when trying to spell unknown words in more than three statements.	✔	All words are decodable and logical in terms of phonics except two: 'favroit' for 'favourite' and 'exsersed' for 'exhausted'. This may be connected to the way he speaks.
21	Can usually use a capital letter and full stop, question mark or exclamation mark to punctuate sentences.	●	There are often no capitals after full stops.
22	Can produce a paragraph or more of developed ideas independently that can be read without help from the child.	✔	This is a good example.

Assessment score

0–6 ticks = not yet working at this Standard; review against Standard 1.
7–12 ticks = Developing   13–17 ticks = Secure   18–22 ticks = Advanced
Assessment point: children with 20 or more ticks may be assessed against Standard 3.

Score = 17/21 (1 criterion not assessable so thresholds must be lowered by 1).
Judgement = Standard 2S.

Ryan   Standard 3: Year 2

No	Criteria	Evidence?	Notes
1	Can communicate ideas and meaning confidently in a series of sentences of at least a paragraph in length. (May not be accurate, but mainly 'flows'.)	✔	Length and 'flow' are both good.
2	Can control use of ascenders/descenders and upper/lower case letters in handwriting.	●	Writing is becoming neat and controlled, but use of capitals and ascenders/descenders are not always secure.
3	Can write in three or more text forms with reasonable accuracy.	✔	This is a letter, so it can be assumed that all three early text forms from Year 1 are also secure.
4	Can provide enough detail to interest the reader.	✔	The opening paragraphs have a good, 'chatty' tone that conveys enthusiasm for the visit.
5	Can vary the structure of sentences to interest the reader (e.g. questions, direct speech or opening with a subordinate clause, etc.).	✘	There is no evidence of this.
6	Can sometimes use interesting and ambitious words (they should be words not usually used by a child of that age, and not a technical word used in a taught context only).	●	'extraordinary', 'persuade', 'special' are interesting words but they are not 'WOW' words for a 9 year old.
7	Can usually sustain narrative and non-narrative forms (can write at length – close to a side of A4 at least – staying on task).	●	Handwriting is oversized, which gives this a feeling of being longer than it is. One more good paragraph is needed.
8	Can match organization to purpose.	✔	The letter structure is secure (NB: the address has been removed for publication).
9	Can usually maintain the use of basic sentence punctuation (full stops followed by capital letters) in a piece close to a side of A4 in length.	●	The first four sentences are accurately punctuated, but then it becomes weaker - usually through missing capital letters after the full stops.
10	Can spell most common words correctly and most of the Years R, 1 & 2 High Frequency Words, and the Year 1 & 2 words in the N.C. Appendix 1.	●	Early words like 'best', 'to', 'will' and 'what' etc. are incorrect.
11	Can use phonetically plausible strategies to spell or attempt to spell unknown polysyllabic words.	✔	All spellings are logical and decodable.
12	Can use connectives other than 'and' to join two or more simple sentences, thoughts, ideas, etc. (e.g. but, so, then, or, when, if, that, because).	✔	'if', 'and', 'before' are secure; 'but' is used slightly incorrectly.
13	Can use a range of punctuation, mainly correctly, including at least three of the following: full stop and capital letter, exclamation mark, question mark, comma (at least in lists), apostrophe for simple contraction and for singular possession (at least).	✘	The punctuation is weak. Full stops and capital letters are not maintained throughout plus there is only one exclamation mark.
14	Can make their writing lively and interesting (e.g. provides additional detail, consciously uses humour, varies sentence length or uses punctuation to create effect, etc.).	●	The 'voice' in the first half is interesting, but there is no variation in sentence structure, additional detail, humour or punctuation for effect (other than one exclamation mark).
15	Can link ideas and events, using strategies to create 'flow'.	●	'Before'
16	Can use adjectives and descriptive phrases for detail and emphasis (consciously selects the adjective for purpose).	✔	E.g. 'extraordinary', 'own', 'greatest', 'special'.
17	Structures basic sentences correctly, including capitals and full stops in a longer piece (one error is acceptable).	●	First four sentences only are accurate.
18	Can use accurate and consistent handwriting (in print at a minimum, can show consistent use of upper/lower case, ascenders/descenders, size and form).	✘	Writing is becoming neat and controlled, but use of capitals and ascenders/descenders are not always secure.
19	Begins to show evidence of joined handwriting.	✔	Writing is almost totally joined.
20	Uses past and present tenses correctly.	✔	Tense is maintained.
21	Can produce close to a side (or more) of A4 writing that is clear and coherent with one or more strong features.	●	The piece is a little too short. There are no strong features other than the enthusiasm in the opening.

Assessment score

0–5 ticks = not yet working at this Standard; review against Standard 2
6–9 ticks = Developing   10–16 ticks = Secure   17–21 ticks = Advanced
Assessment point: children with 18 or more ticks may be assessed against Standard 4.

Score = 9/21.   Judgement = Standard 3D.

James   Standard 4: Year 3

No	Criteria	Evidence?	Notes
1	Can produce work which is organized, imaginative and clear (e.g. simple opening and ending).	✔	The writing uses a letter structure and paragraphs for organization, contains imaginative description (if a little overdone at times) and a clear structure.
2	Can usually join their handwriting.	✔	Writing is all joined.
3	Can use a range of chosen forms appropriately and consistently.	✔	This is a letter, so it can be assumed that all three early text forms from Year 1 are also secure.
4	Can adapt their chosen form to the audience (e.g. provide information about characters or setting, make a series of points, use brackets etc.).	✔	Letter structure / paragraphs to organize.
5	Can sometimes use interesting and ambitious words (they should be words not usually used by a child of that age, and not a technical word used in a taught context only.	●	'inform', 'fantastic', 'flabbergasted'. ('camouflage' is a technical word and was used by all the children).
6	Can develop and extend ideas logically in sequenced sentences (but they may still be overly detailed or brief).	✔	This is secure.
7	Can extend sentences using a wider range of connectives to clarify relationships between points and ideas (e.g. when, because, if, after, while, also, as well).	✔	Uses simple connectives, plus: 'about', 'because', 'after'.
8	Can usually use correct grammatical structures in sentences (nouns and verbs generally agree).	✔	The writing is grammatically correct, although the use of adverbs is slightly awkward at times.
9	Can use pronouns appropriately to avoid the awkward repetition of nouns.	✔	This is secure, e.g. 'our', 'we', 'I', 'you', 'they', etc.
10	Can use most punctuation accurately, including at least three of the following: full stop and capital letter, question mark, exclamation mark, comma, apostrophe.	✔	Writing uses full stops, commas, exclamation marks.
11	Can structure and organize work clearly (e.g. beginning, middle, end; letter structure; dialogue structure).	✔	A letter with paragraphs.
12	Is beginning to use paragraphs.	✔	This is secure.
13	Can adapt form and style for purpose (e.g. there is a clear difference between formal and informal letters; use of abbreviated sentences in notes and diaries, etc.).	✔	It is a factual report within a letter.
14	Can write neatly, legibly and accurately, mainly in a joined style.	●	Handwriting is confident, but a little 'untidy'.
15	Can use adjectives and adverbs for description.	✔	This is secure, but a few adverbs are not used quite correctly or are not quite appropriate in the context.
16	Can spell phonetically regular, or familiar common polysyllabic words accurately and most or all of the Year 3 High Frequency Words and the Year 3 words in the N.C. Appendix 1.	✔	Very good overall. Errors: 'exitedly', 'definetly',
17	Can develop characters and describe settings, feelings and/or emotions, etc.	●	The third paragraph is a good example of developed description, but there could be a little more detail in places.
18	Can link and relate events, including past, present and future, sensibly (afterwards, before, also, after a while, eventually, etc.).	✔	This is secure, e.g. 'Firstly...', 'After that...', 'Once...', 'Next...', etc.
19	Can attempt to give opinion, interest or humour through detail.	✔	Gives his own opinion on the overall trip, in his response to some things he saw and learned and in his preferences.
20	Can use generalizing words for style (e.g. sometimes, never, always, often, etc.) and/or modal verbs/the conditional tense (e.g. might do it, may go).	●	'something'
21	Is beginning to develop a sense of pace (writing is lively and interesting).	●	The writing could be livelier or express more emotion.

Assessment score

0–5 ticks = not yet working at this Standard; review against Standard 3.
6–9 ticks = Developing   10–17 ticks = Secure   18–21 ticks = Advanced
Assessment point: children with 19 or more ticks may be assessed against Standard 5.

Score = 16/21.   Judgement = Standard 4S.

Anya   Standard 5: Year 4

No	Criteria	Evidence?	Notes
1	Can write in a lively and coherent style.	✔	Writing is lively and clear.
2	Can use a range of styles and genres confidently and independently. (If the writing is a narrative, simple report or recount of a known story this cannot be ticked.)	✔	Letter structure and paragraphing are correct so it can be assumed that all three early text forms from Year 1 are also secure.
3	Can sometimes use interesting and ambitious words (they should be words not usually used by a child of that age, and not a technical word used in a taught context only).	●	'flickering' plus one attempt at 'frantically' used incorrectly.
4	Can organize ideas appropriately for both purpose and reader (e.g. captions, headings, bullets, fonts, chapters, letter formats, paragraphs, etc.).	●	Letter structure with paragraphs but without an address. Includes a P.S. although it is not correctly placed.
5	Can use a wide range of punctuation mainly accurately, including at least three of the following: full stop and capital letter, question mark, exclamation mark, apostrophe and comma.	✔	Punctuation used: comma, exclamation mark, full stop, apostrophe. Commas and apostrophes have also been missed.
6	Can write neatly, legibly and accurately, usually maintaining a joined style.	✔	Neat and mainly joined.
7	Can use more sophisticated connectives (e.g. although, however, nevertheless, despite, contrary to, as well as, etc.).	●	'However…'
8	Can use links to show time and cause.	✔	E.g. 'Firstly…', 'On World Book Day…', 'After that…'.
9	Can open sentences in a wide range of ways for interest and impact.	✔	E.g. 'Firstly…', 'However…', 'After that…', 'When…', 'Frantically…' and 'Smiling…' (The last two are not quite used accurately).
10	Can use paragraphs, although they may not always be accurate.	✔	Paragraphs are mainly well managed.
11	Can produce thoughtful and considered writing (uses simple explanation, opinion, justification and deduction).	✔	The writing opens with an explanation and context. There is opinion in the third and fourth paragraphs and humour in the fifth paragraph ('…and then my chair had…').
12	Can use or attempt grammatically complex structures (e.g. expansion before and after the noun: 'The little, old man who lived on the hill…'; subordinate clauses: 'I felt better when…', etc.).	●	There is developing use of Power Openers, but they are not punctuated and the choices are often not quite right.
13	Can spell unfamiliar regular polysyllabic words accurately and most or all of the Year 4 High Frequency Words and the Year 4 words in the N.C. Appendix 1.	●	There are five errors: 'favourite', 'character', 'then', 'frizzy', 'ponies'.
14	Can use nouns, pronouns and tenses accurately and consistently throughout.	●	'a' is missing on the first line /'…me and Harley…'/'… meet you and if I can go…', 'I seen that…'
15	Can use apostrophes and/or inverted commas, mainly accurately. (If direct speech is not appropriate to the task, apostrophes alone can score the tick).	●	One apostrophe used and one missed. Direct speech used, but not punctuated at all.
16	Can select from a range of known adventurous vocabulary for a purpose, with some words being particularly well chosen.	✘	There is no evidence.
17	Can select interesting strategies to move a piece of writing forward (e.g. asides, characterization, dialogue with the audience, dialogue, etc.).	✘	There is no evidence.
18	Can advise assertively, although not confrontationally, in factual writing (e.g. 'An important thing to think about before deciding…', etc.).	✔	E.g. '…but she didn't like it more than me!', 'This year was the best World Book Day I had yet!'
19	Can develop ideas in creative and interesting ways.	●	The developing skills will soon become strengths with good teaching.

Assessment score

0–5 ticks = not yet working at this Standard; review against Standard 4.
6–9 ticks = Developing   10–15 ticks = Secure   16–19 ticks = Advanced
Assessment point: children with 17 or more ticks may be assessed against Standard 6.
Score = 9/19.   Judgement = Standard 5D.

Emily   Standard 6: Year 5

No	Criteria	Evidence?	Notes
1	Can produce well-structured and organized writing using a range of conventions in layout.	✔	Letter structure, paragraphing and bullets are accurate, although not all sub-paragraphs have a capital letter to open.
2	Can use appropriate informal and formal styles with confidence.	✔	Conversational tone is strong in the opening paragraph. There is a more factual tone in the job descriptions.
3	Can select the correct genre for audience and purpose, and use it accurately.	✔	Good use of a hybrid text, with an information text through lists within a letter.
4	Can select from a wide range of known imaginative and ambitious vocabulary (they should be words that are not usually used by a child of that age) and use them precisely.	✔	'phenomenal', 'exceptional', 'includes', 'requires', 'scrutinize', 'designate'.
5	Can use paragraphs consistently and appropriately.	✔	Paragraphing is used accurately.
6	Can group things appropriately before or after a main verb.	✘	The writer has not created an opportunity for this.
7	Can use all grammar accurately except when consciously using dialect or colloquialism for purpose and audience.	✔	Accurate.
8	Can use different techniques to open or conclude work appropriately.	●	Uses a casual question to open but a standard ending.
9	Can use complex sentence structures appropriately.	●	The type of text does not lend itself well to this, but the sentence opening 'However...' is an example.
10	Can use a wider range of punctuation, almost always accurately, to include three or more of the following: comma, apostrophe, bullets, inverted commas, hyphen, brackets, colon or semi-colon.	✔	Punctuation used: comma, question mark, full stop, apostrophe, colon, bullets, dash (there is one apostrophe missing).
11	Can use punctuation appropriately to create effect.	●	Only uses the question mark.
12	Can write neatly, legibly and accurately in a flowing, joined style.	✔	Handwriting is neat, joined and easily read.
13	Can adapt handwriting for a range of tasks and purposes, including for effect.	✘	No opportunity is created.
14	Can spell accurately in all but the most complex words and most or all of the Year 5 High Frequency Words and the Year 5 words in the N.C. Appendix 1.	✔	Very good spelling. One error = 'exeptional'.
15	Can use the passive voice for variety and to shift focus.	✘	No evidence.
16	Can use a range of narrative techniques with confidence, interweaving elements when appropriate.	✘	The task did not lend itself to this easily, but the writer could have extended the opening to create more opportunities.
17	Can vary sentence length and word order confidently to sustain interest.	●	The short sentences in this piece are mainly due to presentation of information, not a literary technique.
18	Can use a range of devices to adapt writing to the needs of the reader.	✔	There is an introductory paragraph to set the context, bullets and a list with sub-headings.
19	Can use literary features to create effect.	✘	The writer would have had to create an opportunity for this, but could have in a more extended opening or ending.
20	Can interweave implicit and explicit links between sections.	✔	'Anyway', 'when...', 'because', 'However...', 'Beforehand...' are all explicit links. '...should miss out this exceptional opportunity and...' refers back, as does the ending (implicit links).
21	Can use punctuation to show division between clauses, to indicate, to vary pace, to create atmosphere or to sub-divide.	●	Existing punctuation is mainly accurate, but the sub-headings should all have opened with a capital letter. Opportunities were missed for ellipsis and possible brackets.
22	Can show confident and established 'voice'.	●	The piece is mainly confident, but opportunities for many higher Standard features have been missed.

Assessment score

0–7 ticks = not yet working at this Standard; review against Standard 5.
8–11 ticks = Developing   12–18 ticks = Secure   19–22 ticks = Advanced
Assessment point: children with 20 or more ticks may be assessed against Standard 7.

Score = 13/22.   Judgement = Standard 6 Secure.

Leo   Standard 7: Year 6

No	Criteria	Evidence?	Notes
1	Can spell all vocabulary correctly apart from rare technical or obscure words.	●	Errors: 'ajoining', 'sicerely', 'inoccent'.
2	Can open and close writing in interesting, unusual or dramatic ways, when appropriate.	✔	Opens with a scream and ends with a rhetorical question.
3	Can use the full range of punctuation accurately and precisely, including for sub-division, effect, listing, direct speech, parenthesis, etc.	●	Punctuation used: exclamation mark, semi-colon, comma, dash, question mark, apostrophe, brackets, speech marks – all used well except for two small errors with the semi-colons and missed punctuation within the sentences.
4	Can write neatly, legibly, accurately and fluently, in a joined style.	✔	Handwriting is very good, confident, clear and flows.
5	Can vary font for effect or emphasis when appropriate.	✔	There is capitalization for emphasis in the opening shout.
6	Can use a wide range of conventions appropriately to the context, e.g. paragraphs, sub and side headings, addendum, footnote, contents, etc.	✔	E.g. Paragraphs, diary headings, opening with context. No more is required in this piece.
7	Can use a wide range of sophisticated connectives, including conjunctions, adverbs and prepositions, to show time, cause, sequence and mode, including to open sentences sometimes.	✔	Writing uses most of the standard connectives, plus: 'Being...', 'furthermore', 'consequently', 'moreover', 'unfortunately', 'as though', 'until', 'as a result of this'.
8	Can use clauses confidently and appropriately for audience and purpose.	●	This is mainly good, but there are small errors in internal punctuation and some slightly awkward sentences.
9	Can use implicit links within a text, e.g. referring back to a point made earlier or forward to more information or detail to come.	●	Writing is very coherent, referring constantly to the situation they are in and how much he hates it. However, there are no clear, implicit links back to an earlier point.
10	Can use complex groupings for effect, before or after the verb.	✔	There is a complex grouping describing activities in the kitchen.
11	Can use a range of techniques to interact or show awareness of the audience, e.g. action, dialogue, quotation, aside, suspense, tension, comment.	✔	The whole piece is clearly written in a conversational tone and shows sustained awareness of the reader, but also contains dialogue with the audience: action in the opening of Day 2, quotation of his parents and the use of brackets.
12	Can write with maturity, confidence and imagination.	✔	This is a very mature piece for an eleven year old.
13	Can adapt writing for the full range of purposes, always showing awareness of audience.	●	Writing shows consistent awareness of the audience. Could possibly have included more detailed description of one feature, or a wider range of literary features.
14	Can consciously vary levels of formality according to purpose and audience.	✗	There is no evidence.
15	Can sustain a convincing viewpoint throughout the piece of writing.	✔	Quoting parents gives an opposing opinion. The viewpoint of the diary writer is consistent throughout.
16	Can use a wide range of ambitious vocabulary accurately and precisely (they should be words that are not usually used by a child of that age).	✔	E.g. 'Basically', 'saunter', 'adjoining', 'adamant', 'humdrum', 'furthermore', 'enclosed', 'hilarious', 'ventured', etc.
17	Can use two or more stylistic features to create effect within the text.	✔	E.g. rhetorical question, simile, personification, metaphor, three groupings, universal appeal (in the last plea).
18	Can use creative and varied sentence structures when appropriate, intermingling with simple structures for effect.	●	Uses a wide range of sentence openings and expanded noun phrases. Could have included more detailed description of a character, setting or action.
19	Can always construct grammatically correct sentences, unless using dialect or alternative constructions consciously for effect.	✔	There are no grammatical errors, unless intentional.
20	Can use pertinent and precise detail as appropriate.	●	Could have included a more detailed description of a character or setting.
21	Can demonstrate a wide range of the criteria in Standard 7 effectively and in a well-managed and mature way.	●	12 out of 21.

Assessment score

0–6 ticks = not yet working at this Standard; review against Standard 6.
7–10 ticks = Developing   11–17 ticks = Secure   18–21 ticks = Advanced
Score = 12/21   Judgement = Standard 7 Secure

The Oxford Writing Criterion Scale and UK National Curricula

The **Oxford Writing Criterion Scale** (OWCS) describes the detailed steps children make as they learn to write, and presents this information in a format that is specifically designed to facilitate consistent summative assessment. It represents the skills hierarchy common to all children's development regardless of curriculum, and it therefore provides a robust assessment tool alongside any curriculum. Recently, some additions and adaptations have been made to the OWCS in order to ensure that it supports specifically all the expectations in the National Curriculum for England from 2014 but in terms of content and expectations there remains an excellent correlation to other UK curricula. The sections that follow explain how the OWCS fits with the requirements of the various UK curricula.

The Oxford Writing Criterion Scale and the curriculum in England

The Early Years Foundation Stage Writing

Statutory requirements: children use their phonic knowledge to write words in ways which match their spoken sounds. They also write some irregular common words. They write simple sentences which can be read by themselves and others. Some words are spelt correctly and others are phonetically plausible.

The chart below is based on Development Matters – non-statutory guidance material which fleshes out the statutory requirements of the EYFS and supports practitioners in implementing them.

Development Matters Guidelines: 30 to 50 months	Oxford Writing Criterion Scale link
Sometimes gives meaning to marks as they draw and paint.	Pre Writing Standard: 6, 7, 15, 16
Ascribes meanings to marks that they see in different places.	Pre Writing Standard: 8, 14, 18
Development Matters Guidelines: 40 to 60+ months	**Oxford Writing Criterion Scale link**
Gives meaning to marks they make as they draw, write and paint.	Pre-Writing Standard: 11, 13, 15, 16
Uses some clearly identifiable letters to communicate meaning, representing some sounds correctly and in sequence.	Pre-Writing Standard: 9, 16, 17 Standard 1: 1
Writes own name and other things such as labels, captions.	Pre-Writing Standard: 17 Standard1: 2, 5, 11
Attempts to write short sentences in meaningful contexts.	Standard 1: 3, 12, 13, 14, 19

By the end of the Reception Year children should be a Secure Standard 1 on the Oxford Writing Criterion Scale to be in line with National Curriculum expectations.

Appendix 3: The OWCS and the Curriculum in England

Year 1 Programme of Study for Writing

TRANSCRIPTION National Curriculum objective	Oxford Writing Criterion Scale link
Pupils should be taught to:	
Spell:	
words containing each of the 40+ phonemes already taught	**Standard 2: 6, 13**
common exception words	**Standard 2: 13**
the days of the week	**Standard 2: 13**
Name the letters of the alphabet:	**Standard 2: 2**
naming the letters of the alphabet in order	**Standard 1: 4**
using letter names to distinguish between alternative spellings of the same sound	**Standard 2: 5, 14, 20**
Add prefixes and suffixes:	**Standard 2: 18**
apply simple spelling rules and guidelines	**Standard 1: 9, 10, 15, 18** **Standard 2: 5, 6, 13**
write from memory simple sentences dictated by the teacher that include words using the GPCs and common exception words taught so far	**Standard 2: 7, 6, 13, 15**
HANDWRITING **National Curriculum objective**	**Oxford Writing Criterion Scale link**
Pupils should be taught to:	
sit correctly at a table, holding a pencil comfortably and correctly	**Standard 1: 8**
begin to form lower-case letters in the correct direction, starting and finishing in the right place	**Standard 2: 1, 8, 17**
form capital letters	**Standard 2: 1, 8, 17**
COMPOSITION **National Curriculum objective**	**Oxford Writing Criterion Scale link**
Pupils should be taught to write sentences by:	
saying out loud what they are going to write about.	**Standard 2: 11**
composing a sentence orally before writing it.	**Standard 1: 17**
sequencing sentences to form short narratives.	**Standard 2: 18, 22**
re-reading what they have written to check that it makes sense.	**Standard 2: 9, 11**
discuss what they have written with the teacher or other pupils.	**Standard 2: 9**
read aloud their writing clearly enough to be heard by their peers and the teacher .	**Standard 2: 9**
VOCABULARY, GRAMMAR AND PUNCTUATION **National Curriculum objective**	**Oxford Writing Criterion Scale link**
Pupils should be taught to develop their understanding of the concepts set out in Appendix 2 by:	
leaving spaces between words	**Standard 1: 12** **Standard 2: 4**
joining words and joining clauses using 'and'	**Standard 2: 18**
beginning to punctuate sentences using a capital letter and a full stop, question mark or exclamation mark	**Standard 2: 16, 17, 21**
using a capital letter for names of people, places, the days of the week, and the personal pronoun 'I'	**Standard 2: 1, 21**

By the end of Year 1 children should be a Secure Standard 2 on the Oxford Writing Criterion Scale to be in line with National Curriculum expectations.

Year 2 Programme of Study for Writing

TRANSCRIPTION National Curriculum objective	Oxford Writing Criterion Scale link
Pupils should be taught to:	
spell by:	
segmenting spoken words into phonemes and representing these by graphemes, spelling many correctly	**Standard 3: 10, 11**
learning new ways of spelling phonemes for which one or more spellings are already known, and learn some words with each spelling, including a few common homophones	**Standard 3: 10, 11**
learning to spell common exception words	**Standard 3: 10**
learning to spell more words with contracted forms	**Standard 3: 11, 13**
learning the possessive apostrophe (singular) [for example, the girl's book]	**Standard 3: 13**
add suffixes to spell longer words, e.g. –ment, –ness, –ful, -less, -ly	**Standard 3: 11**
apply spelling rules and guidelines	**Standard 3: 10, 11**
write from memory simple sentences dictated by the teacher that include words and punctuation taught so far	**Standard 3: 3, 21**
HANDWRITING National Curriculum objective	**Oxford Writing Criterion Scale link**
Pupils should be taught to:	
form lower-case letters of the correct size relative to one another	**Standard 3: 2, 18**
start using some of the diagonal and horizontal strokes needed to join letters and understand which letters, when adjacent to one another, are best left unjoined	**Standard 3: 19**
write capital letters and digits of the correct size, orientation and relationship to one another and to lower case letters	**Standard 3:2, 17, 18**
use spacing between words that reflects the size of the letters	**Standard 3: 2, 17, 18**
COMPOSITION National Curriculum objective	**Oxford Writing Criterion Scale link**
Pupils should be taught to:	
develop positive attitudes towards and stamina for writing by:	
writing narratives about personal experiences and those of others (real and fictional)	**Standard 3: 1, 3, 7**
writing about real events	**Standard 3: 1, 3, 7**
writing poetry	**Standard 3: 1, 3, 7, 16**
writing for different purposes	**Standard 3: 1, 3, 7, 8, 14**
consider what they are going to write before beginning by encapsulating what they want to say, sentence by sentence	**Standard 3: 1, 5, 7, 8, 9, 12, 15**
make simple additions, revisions and corrections to their own writing by re-reading to check that their writing makes sense and that verbs to indicate time are used correctly and consistently, including verbs in the continuous form	**Standard 3: 20**
read aloud what they have written with appropriate intonation to make the meaning clear	**Standard 3: 1, 15**
VOCABULARY, GRAMMAR AND PUNCTUATION National Curriculum objective	**Oxford Writing Criterion Scale link**
Pupils should be taught to: develop their understanding of the concepts set out in Appendix 2 by:	
learning how to use both familiar and new punctuation correctly, including full stops, capital letters, exclamation marks, question marks, commas for lists and apostrophes for contracted forms *and the possessive singular*	**Standard 3: 9, 13, 17, 20**
learn how to use:	
sentences with different forms: statement, question, exclamation, command	**Standard 3: 3, 5, 7, 8, 12, 17**
expanded noun phrases to describe and specify, e.g. the blue butterfly	**Standard 3: 4, 6, 14, 16**
the present and past tenses correctly and consistently including the progressive form	**Standard 3: 20**
subordination (using when, if, that, or because) and co-ordination (using or, and, or but)	**Standard 3: 12, 15**
some features of written Standard English	**Standard 3: 12, 13, 20, 21**

By the end of Year 2 children should be a Secure Standard 3 on the Oxford Writing Criterion Scale to be in line with National Curriculum expectations.

Year 3 and 4 Programme of Study for Writing

TRANSCRIPTION National Curriculum objective	Oxford Writing Criterion Scale link
Pupils should be taught to:	
spell further homophones	**Standard 5: 13**
spell words that are often misspelt	**Standard 5:13**
place the possessive apostrophe accurately in words with regular plurals [for example, girls', boys'] and in words with irregular plurals [for example, children's]	**Standard 5: 15**
write from memory simple sentences, dictated by the teacher, that include words and punctuation taught so far.	**Standard 5: 5, 6, 13, 14, 15**
HANDWRITING **National Curriculum objective**	**Oxford Writing Criterion Scale link**
Pupils should be taught to:	
use the diagonal and horizontal strokes that are needed to join letters and understand which letters, when adjacent to one another, are best left unjoined	**Standard 4: 2, 14** **Standard 5: 6**
increase the legibility, consistency and quality of their handwriting, e.g. by ensuring that the downstrokes of letters are parallel and equidistant; that lines of writing are spaced sufficiently so that the ascenders and descenders of letters do not touch	**Standard 4: 2, 14** **Standard 5: 6**
COMPOSITION **National Curriculum objective**	**Oxford Writing Criterion Scale link**
Pupils should be taught to:	
plan their writing by:	
discussing writing similar to that which they are planning to write in order to understand and learn from its structure, vocabulary and grammar	**Standard 5: 2, 3, 4, 9, 12, 16**
discussing and recording ideas	**Standard 4: 1, 4, 6, 7, 11, 13** **Standard 5: 1, 3, 4, 10, 19**
draft and write by:	
composing and rehearsing sentences orally (including dialogue), progressively building a varied and rich vocabulary and an increasing range of sentence structures	**Standard 4: 5, 6, 7, 11** **Standard 5: 1, 2, 3, 7, 9, 12, 16, 17, 18**
organising paragraphs around a theme	**Standard 4: 11, 12** **Standard 5: 4, 10, 17**
in narratives, creating settings, characters and plot	**Standard 4: 4, 17, 18** **Standard 5: 4, 8, 17, 19**
in non-narrative material, using simple organisational devices such as headings and sub-headings	**Standard 4: 1, 3, 11, 13** **Standard 5: 2, 4**
evaluate and edit by:	
assessing the effectiveness of their own and others' writing and suggesting improvements	**Standard 5: 11, 16, 17, 18, 19**
proposing changes to grammar and vocabulary to improve consistency, e.g. the accurate use of pronouns in sentences	**Standard 5: 3, 5, 9, 14, 16**

Year 3 and 4 Programme of Study for Writing

VOCABULARY, GRAMMAR AND PUNCTUATION National Curriculum objective	Oxford Writing Criterion Scale link
Pupils should be taught to:	
develop their understanding by:	
extending the range of sentences with more than one clause by using a wider range of conjunctions, e.g. when, if, because, although	**Standard 4: 7** **Standard 5: 7, 12, 18**
using the perfect form of verbs to mark relationships of time and cause	**Standard 4: 18, 20** **Standard 5: 8, 14**
choosing nouns or pronouns appropriately for clarity and cohesion and to avoid repetition	**Standard 4: 9** **Standard 5: 12, 14**
using conjunctions, adverbs and prepositions to express time and cause	**Standard 4: 7, 18, 20** **Standard 5: 4, 7, 8, 12, 14**
using fronted adverbials	**Standard 4: 20** **Standard 5: 7, 9, 12, 18**
indicate grammatical and other features by:	
using commas after fronted adverbials	**Standard 4: 10** **Standard 5: 5, 9, 15, 18**
indicating possession by using the possessive apostrophe with singular and plural nouns	**Standard 4: 8, 10** **Standard 5: 5, 15**
using and punctuating direct speech	**Standard 4: 10** **Standard 5: 15**

By the end of Year 3 children should be a Secure Standard 4 on the Oxford Writing Criterion Scale to be in line with National Curriculum expectations.

By the end of Year 4 children should be a Secure Standard 5 on the Oxford Writing Criterion Scale to be in line with National Curriculum expectations.

Year 5 and 6 Programme of Study for Writing

TRANSCRIPTION National Curriculum objective	Oxford Writing Criterion Scale link
Pupils should be taught to:	
spell some words with 'silent' letters, e.g. knight, psalm, solemn	**Standard 6: 4, 14**
continue to distinguish between homophones and other words which are often confused	**Standard 6: 14**
use knowledge of morphology and etymology in spelling and understand that the spelling of some words needs to be learnt specifically	**Standard 6:14**

HANDWRITING National Curriculum objective	Oxford Writing Criterion Scale link
Pupils should be taught to write legibly, fluently and with increasing speed by:	
choosing which shape of a letter to use when given choices and deciding, as part of their personal style, whether or not to join specific letters	**Standard 6: 1, 12, 13** **Standard 7: 4, 5**

COMPOSITION National Curriculum objective	Oxford Writing Criterion Scale link
Pupils should be taught to:	
plan their writing by:	
identifying the audience for and purpose of the writing, selecting the appropriate form and using other similar writing as models for their own	**Standard 6: 1, 2, 3, 16, 17** **Standard 7: 6, 8, 11, 13, 14**
in writing narratives, considering how authors have developed characters and settings in what they have read, listened to or seen performed	**Standard 6: 8, 15, 16, 18, 19** **Standard 7: 15**
draft and write by:	
selecting appropriate grammar and vocabulary, understanding how such choices can change and enhance meaning	**Standard 6: 2, 4, 7, 9, 10, 11, 19** **Standard 7: 2, 3, 7, 8, 11, 14, 17, 18, 19**
in narratives, describing settings, characters and atmosphere and integrating dialogue to convey character and advance the action	**Standard 6: 4, 16, 18, 19, 22** **Standard 7: 2, 11, 12, 15, 17**
précising longer passages	**Standard 7: 21**
using a wide range of devices to build cohesion within and across paragraphs	**Standard 6: 6, 8, 20, 21** **Standard 7: 3, 7, 8, 10, 18**
using further organisational and presentational devices to structure text and to guide the reader (e.g. headings, bullet points, underlining)	**Standard 6: 18** **Standard 7: 3, 6, 7**
evaluate and edit by:	
ensuring the consistent and correct use of tense throughout a piece of writing	**Standard 7: 7, 9, 19**
ensuring correct subject and verb agreement when using singular and plural, distinguishing between the language of speech and writing and choosing the appropriate register	**Standard 7: 3, 8, 11, 18, 19**

Year 5 and 6 Programme of Study for Writing

VOCABULARY, GRAMMAR AND PUNCTUATION National Curriculum objective	Oxford Writing Criterion Scale link
Pupils should be taught to:	
develop their understanding by:	
recognising vocabulary and structures that are appropriate for formal speech and writing, including subjunctive forms	**Standard 6: 2, 7, 9, 11, 16** **Standard 7: 6, 7, 8, 11, 12, 13, 14, 19**
using passive verbs to affect the presentation of information in a sentence	**Standard 6: 15** **Standard 7: 7, 8, 10, 12, 18**
using the perfect form of verbs to mark relationships of time and cause	**Standard 7: 7, 19**
using expanded noun phrases to convey complicated information concisely	**Standard 6: 6, 15, 17** **Standard 7: 7, 8, 10, 18**
using modal verbs or adverbs to indicate degrees of possibility	**Standard 6: 8, 17** **Standard 7: 7, 9**
using relative clauses beginning with who, which, where, when, whose, that or with an implied (i.e. omitted) relative pronoun	**Standard 6** **Standard 7: 7, 18, 19**
indicate grammatical and other features by:	
using commas to clarify meaning or avoid ambiguity in writing	**Standard 6: 10, 11, 17, 21** **Standard 7: 3, 19**
using hyphens to avoid ambiguity	**Standard 6: 10, 11, 21** **Standard 7: 3, 6**
using brackets, dashes or commas to indicate parenthesis	**Standard 6: 10, 11, 18, 21** **Standard 7: 3**
using semi-colons, colons or dashes to mark boundaries between main clauses	**Standard 6: 21** **Standard 7: 3, 19**
using a colon to introduce a list	**Standard 6: 10, 11, 21** **Standard 7: 3, 19**

By the end of Year 5 children should be a Secure Standard 6 on the Oxford Writing Criterion Scale to be in line with National Curriculum expectations.

By the end of Year 6 children should be a Secure Standard 7 on the Oxford Writing Criterion Scale to be in line with National Curriculum expectations.

The Oxford Writing Criterion Scale and the Scottish Curriculum for Excellence

Early Level Writing

Tools for writing	Oxford Writing Criterion Scale link
I explore sounds, letters and words, discovering how they work together, and I can use what I learn to help me as I read or write. (ENG 0-12a / LIT 0-13a / LIT 0-21a)	**Standard 1: 1, 3, 4**
As I play and learn, I enjoy exploring interesting materials for writing and different ways of recording my experiences and feelings, ideas and information. (LIT 0-21b)	**Standard 1: 3, 8, 16, 17**
Organising and using information	
Within real and imaginary situations, I share experiences and feelings, ideas and information in a way that communicates my message. (LIT 0-26a)	**Standard 1: 14, 17**
Creating texts	
I enjoy exploring events and characters in stories and other texts and I use what I learn to invent my own, sharing these with others in imaginative ways. (LIT 0-09b / LIT 0-31a)	**Standard 1: 14, 16**

First Level Writing

Enjoyment and choice	Oxford Writing Criterion Scale link
I enjoy creating texts of my choice and I regularly select subject, purpose, format and resources to suit the needs of my audience. (LII 1-20a / LIT 2-20a)	**Standard 2: 7, 15, 19** **Standard 3: 3, 4, 8, 14, 16** **Standard 4: 1, 3, 4, 13, 19, 21**
Tools for writing	
I can spell the most commonly-used words, using my knowledge of letter patterns and spelling rules and use resources to help me spell tricky or unfamiliar words. (LIT 1-21a)	**Standard 2: 3, 5, 6, 13, 20** **Standard 3: 10** **Standard 4: 16**
I can write independently, use appropriate punctuation and order and link my sentences in a way that makes sense. (LIT 1-22a)	**Standard 2: 1, 2, 3, 4, 8, 15, 21, 22** **Standard 3: 1, 2, 5, 9, 13, 17, 21** **Standard 4: 6, 10, 12**
Throughout the writing process, I can check that my writing makes sense. (LIT 1-23a)	**Standard 2: 15, 17, 18, 20, 21** **Standard 3: 1, 12, 15, 21** **Standard 4: 6, 11, 18, 19, 20, 21**
I can present my writing in a way that will make it legible/attractive for my reader, combining words, images and other features. (LIT 1-24a)	**Standard 2: 2, 8, 17** **Standard 3: 2, 18, 19** **Standard 4: 2, 14**
Organising and using information	
I am learning to use my notes and other types of writing to help me understand information and ideas, explore problems, generate and develop ideas or create new text. (LIT 1-25a)	**Standard 2: 10, 11, 14, 21** **Standard 3: 1, 7, 8, 15, 21** **Standard 4: 1, 3, 11, 12, 21**
By considering the type of text I am creating I can select ideas and relevant information, organise these in a logical sequence and use words which will be interesting and/or useful for others. (LIT 1-26a)	**Standard 2: 7, 14, 18** **Standard 3: 3, 7, 8** **Standard 4: 3, 4, 13**
Creating texts	
I can convey information, describe events or processes, share my opinions or persuade my reader in different ways. (LIT 1-28a / LIT 1-29a)	**Standard 2: 14, 21** **Standard 3: 1, 4, 15, 21** **Standard 4: 1, 4, 13, 19**
I can describe and share my experiences and how they made me feel. (ENG 1-30a)	**Standard 2: 9, 15, 22** **Standard 3: 1, 14, 15, 21** **Standard 4: 1, 6, 13, 17, 18**
Having explored the elements which writers use in different genres, I can use what I learn to create my own stories, poems and plays with interesting structures, characters and/or settings.	**Standard 2: 11, 15, 19, 22** **Standard 3: 3, 7, 14, 16, 17, 21** **Standard 4:3, 4, 13, 15, 17, 18, 19, 21**
Having explored the elements which writers use in different genres, I can use what I learn to create my own stories, poems and plays with interesting structures, characters and/or settings. (ENG 1-31a)	**Standard 2: 7, 15** **Standard 3: 3, 7, 14, 16, 21** **Standard 4: 3, 4, 13, 17, 18, 19, 20, 21**

Second Level Writing

Enjoyment and choice	Oxford Writing Criterion Scale link
I enjoy creating texts of my choice and I regularly select subject, purpose, format and resources to suit the needs of my audience. (LIT 1-20a / LIT 2-20a)	**Standard 5: 2, 3, 9, 16, 17, 19** **Standard 6: 1, 2, 3, 4, 17, 18, 22** **Standard 7: 2, 6, 12, 13, 15, 18, 21**
Tools for writing	
I can spell most of the words I need to communicate, using spelling rules, specialist vocabulary, self-correction techniques and a range of resources. (LIT 2-21a)	**Standard 5: 13** **Standard 6: 14** **Standard 7: 1**
In both short and extended texts, I can use appropriate punctuation, vary my sentence structures and divide my work into paragraphs in a way that makes sense to my reader. (LIT 2-22a)	**Standard 5: 5, 15** **Standard 6: 10, 11, 21** **Standard 7: 3**
Throughout the writing process, I can check that my writing makes sense and meets its purpose. (LIT 2-23a)	**Standard 5: 8, 17, 18** **Standard 6: 2, 9, 20, 21** **Standard 7: 8, 9, 11**
I consider the impact that layout and presentation will have and can combine lettering, graphics and other features to engage my reader. (LIT 2-24a)	**Standard 5: 6, 10** **Standard 6: 1, 4, 11, 12, 13, 18, 21** **Standard 7: 4, 5, 6**
Organising and using information	
I can use my notes and other types of writing to help me understand information and ideas, explore problems, make decisions, generate and develop ideas or create new text. I recognise the need to acknowledge my sources and can do this appropriately. (LIT 2-25a)	**Standard 5: 11, 17, 18** **Standard 6: 1, 8, 16, 22** **Standard 7: 9, 13, 16, 18, 20, 21**
By considering the type of text I am creating, I can select ideas and relevant information, organise these in an appropriate way for my purpose and use suitable vocabulary for my audience. (LIT 2-26a)	**Standard 5: 2, 4, 9, 10** **Standard 6: 2, 3, 5, 17, 18, 19** **Standard 7: 6, 8, 13, 14, 18**
Creating texts	
I am learning to use language and style in a way which engages and/or influences my reader. (ENG 2-27a)	**Standard 5: 1, 2, 3, 7, 9, 11, 16, 17, 19** **Standard 6: 1, 9, 11, 13, 15, 16, 17, 18, 19, 21** **Standard 7: 2, 3, 5, 7, 10, 12, 16, 17, 18, 21**
I can convey information, describe events, explain processes or combine ideas in different ways. (LIT 2-28a)	**Standard 5: 1, 11, 17, 18, 19** **Standard 6: 2, 16** **Standard 7: 2, 6, 12, 15, 20, 21**
I can persuade, argue, explore issues or express an opinion using relevant supporting detail and/or evidence. (IT 2-29a)	**Standard 5: 8, 11, 17, 18, 19** **Standard 6: 8, 16, 22** **Standard 7: 15, 18**
Having explored the elements which writers use in different genres, I can use what I learn to create stories, poems and plays with an interesting and appropriate structure, interesting characters and/or settings which come to life. (ENG 2-31a)	**Standard 5: 2, 3, 11, 16, 19** **Standard 6: 1, 2, 9, 11, 15, 16, 19, 22** **Standard 7: 2, 6, 11, 12, 15, 17, 18, 21**

The Oxford Writing Criterion Scale and the Welsh National Literacy Framework

Nursery

Writing: Organising ideas and discussion Meaning, purposes, readers	Oxford Writing Criterion Scale link
experiment with a range of mark-making materials across a range of contexts	Pre-W: 3, 4, 5, 6
attribute meaning to marks, drawings and art work, e.g. adult anotation	Pre-W: 11, 13
communicate by using symbols and pictures	N/A
write letters, numbers and/or symbols randomly	Pre-W: 6, 7, 8, 15, 16, 17
use pictures to convey meaning on-screen	N/A
Writing: Organising ideas and discussion **Structure and organisation**	
orally contribute to a form modelled by the adult	N/A
Writing accurately: grammar, punctuation, spelling, handwriting	
pick up small objects with finger and thumb and start to hold writing implements appropriately, using pincer grip	Pre-W: 1, 3, 5
demonstrate an understanding of the directionality of written print	Pre-W: 14
identify letter sounds through exploration of their shape using tactile letter forms and multi-sensory play activities	N/A

Reception

Writing: Organising ideas and discussion Meaning, purposes, readers	Oxford Writing Criterion Scale link
compose and dictate a sentence describing events, experiences and pictures to communicate meaning	Standard 1: 14, 17
convey meaning through pictures and mark making	Standard 1: 3
recognise the alphabetic nature of writing and understand that written symbols have meaning	Pre-W: 11
copy and write letters, words and phrases	Standard 1: 1
use pictures and symbols to compose writing on-screen	N/A
Writing: Organising ideas and discussion **Structure and organisation**	
begin to sequence words, signs or symbols appropriately	Pre-W: 9 Standard 1: 4, 5, 13
contribute to a form modelled by the teacher, e.g. through shared writing	Standard 1: 17
show understanding of different formats, e.g. cards, lists, invitations.	Pre-W: 12 Standard 1: 6
Writing accurately: grammar, punctuation, spelling, handwriting	
hold writing instruments appropriately	Standard 1: 8
write from left to right	Pre-W: 9 Standard 1: 2, 13
discriminate between letters	Pre-W: 8
distinguish between upper- and lower-case letters	N/A
use correct initial consonant by beginning to apply phonic knowledge	Pre-w: 15
use familiar and high-frequency words in writing	Standard 1: 2

Year 1

Writing: Organising ideas and discussion Meaning, purposes, readers	Oxford Writing Criterion Scale link
communicate purposefully in writing, e.g. may be supported by a drawing	Standard 1: 19, Standard 2: 10, 15, 22
use pictures, symbols, letters in sequence and familiar words to communicate meaning	Standard 1: 11
talk about what they are going to write	Standard 1: 17
write words, phrases and simple sentences and read back own attempts	Standard 1: 7, 14 Standard 2: 3, 7, 9
select letters, words and pictures to compose writing on-screen	N/A
Writing: Organising ideas and discussion **Structure and organisation**	
sequence content correctly, e.g. instructions, recipes	Standard 2: 12
follow a form modelled by the teacher	Standard 1: 16 Standard 2: 10
understand different types of writing, e.g. records of events, descriptions, narrative	Standard 2: 11, 15
Writing accurately: language	
use specific words which relate to the topic of their writing.	Standard 2: 19
Writing accurately: grammar, punctuation, spelling, handwriting	
form upper- and lower-case letters that are usually clearly shaped and correctly orientated	Standard 2: 1, 2, 8, 17
use capital letters and full stops with some degree of consistency	Standard 2: 16, 21
begin to use connectives to expand a point	Standard 2: 18
spell some words conventionally, including consonant-vowel-consonant and common digraphs, e.g. th, ck	Standard 1: 10 Standard 2: 6
use spelling strategies such as sound–symbol correspondence and segmenting	Standard 2: 5, 14, 20
spell high-frequency words correctly	Standard 1: 9, 15, 18 Standard 2: 13

Year 2

Writing: Organising ideas and discussion Meaning, purposes, readers	
write for different purposes	Standard 3: 2, 7
write text which makes sense to another reader, which may include details and pictures	Standard 3: 1, 4, 5, 21
use talk to plan writing	N/A
re-read and improve their writing to ensure that it makes sense	N/A
experiment with different formats and layouts on-screen, using the facility to move text and pictures around easily	N/A
Writing: Organising ideas and discussion **Structure and organisation**	
follow a structure in their writing with support, e.g. reports, lists	Standard 3: 8
follow and build upon a form modelled by the teacher	Standard 3: 3, 14
organise writing with a beginning, middle and end	Standard 3: 3
use different types of writing appropriate to purpose and reader.	Standard 3: 8
Writing accurately: language	
understand and use language appropriate to writing	Standard 3: 6, 16
use simple subject-related words appropriately.	Standard 3: 16
Writing accurately: grammar, punctuation, spelling, handwriting	
form upper- and lower-case letters accurately and with consistent size	Standard 3: 2, 18
use capital letters, full stops and question marks accurately and sometimes use exclamation marks	Standard 3: 9, 13, 17
use connectives to write compound sentences	Standard 3: 12
use ordering words, e.g. first, next, then, lastly	Standard 3: 15
use standard forms of verbs, e.g. see/saw, go/went, and subject–verb agreement, e.g. I was/we were	Standard 3: 20 Standard 4: 8
use spelling strategies such as segmenting, simple roots and suffixes, e.g. ing, ed	Standard 3: 11
spell high-frequency words correctly	Standard 3: 10

Year 3

Writing: Organising ideas and discussion Meaning, purposes, readers	Oxford Writing Criterion Scale link
write for different purposes and readers choosing words for variety and interest	Standard 4: 3, 4, 5
include relevant details, information or observations in their writing	Standard 4: 17, 19
note down ideas to use in writing	N/A
use on-screen functions, e.g. font, colour, cut, paste, size, to present their work in ways to interest the reader and enhance meaning	N/A
review and improve sections of their work	An expectation from Standard 4 onwards
Writing: Organising ideas and discussion **Structure and organisation**	
use a basic structure for writing	Standard 4: 1, 11
write using an introduction to the topic and a conclusion	Standard 4: 11, 12
present processes, event or reports in a clear sequence	Standard 4: 6
use visual information if relevant, e.g. labelled diagrams	Standard 3: 8 Standard 4: 3, 4
Writing accurately: language	
use language appropriate to writing, including standard forms of English	Standard 4: 13, 20
use vocabulary related to the topic or subject context	Standard 4: 5
Writing accurately: grammar, punctuation, spelling, handwriting	
start sentences in a variety of ways	Standard 4: 18
use adjectives and adverbs to expand simple sentences and phrases	Standard 4: 15
use connectives for causation and consequence, e.g. because, after	Standard 4: 7, 18
use full stops, question marks, exclamation marks and commas for lists	Standard 4: 10
spell plural forms, e.g. -s, -es, -ies	Standard 3: 10, 11 Standard 4: 16
use past tense of verbs consistently, e.g. consonant doubling before ed	Standard 4: 8
use strategies including knowledge of word families, roots, morphology and graphic knowledge to spell words, e.g. most common polysyllabic words	Standard 4: 16
spell all high-frequency words correctly	Standard 4: 16
produce legible handwriting and present work appropriately joining letters in some words	Standard 4: 2, 14

Year 4

Writing: Organising ideas and discussion Meaning, purposes, readers	Oxford Writing Criterion Scale link
adapt what they write to the purpose and reader, choosing words appropriately, e.g. descriptive, persuasive language	Standard 5: 1, 2, 4
explain main idea(s) with supporting details, including observations and explanations where relevant	Standard 5: 11, 19
gather ideas to plan writing	N/A
explore and use appropriately the different forms of writing on-screen to interact with others, e.g. websites, e-mails, blogs	N/A
improve writing, checking for clarity and organisation	An expectation from Standard 4 onwards
Writing: Organising ideas and discussion Structure and organisation	
use specific structures in writing, e.g. tables, questionnaires	Standard 5: 4
write an introduction, develop a series of ideas and a conclusion	Standard 5: 8, 9, 11
organise writing into logical sequences or sections by beginning to use paragraphs	Standard 5: 10
use visual information, e.g. illustrations, diagrams and graphs, which are clear and relevant to the written text.	N/A
Writing accurately: language	
use language appropriate to writing, including standard forms of English	Standard 5: 3, 16
use subject-specific vocabulary independently.	Standard 5: 3, 16
Writing accurately: grammar, punctuation, spelling, handwriting	
vary the order of words, phrases and clauses in sentences	Standard 5: 9
use adjectival and adverbial phrases to add interest and precision	Standard 5: 12
use connectives to show links within sentences	Standard 5: 7, 8
use punctuation to demarcate sentences and begin to use speech marks, commas to mark clauses and phrases, and apostrophes for omission, e.g. it's (it is)	Standard 5: 5, 15
use strategies including knowledge of word families, roots, morphology, derivations and graphic knowledge to spell words, e.g. words with more complex patterns	Standard 5: 13
produce handwriting which is clear and legible and may be cursive	Standard 5: 6

Year 5

Writing: Organising ideas and discussion Meaning, purposes, readers	Oxford Writing Criterion Scale link
write with a clear purpose, showing consideration for the reader, e.g. by choosing appropriate vocabulary and presentational devices	Standard 6: 1, 3, 4, 18
expand upon main idea(s) with supporting reasons, information and examples	Standard 6: 9
use techniques in planning writing, e.g. mindmapping, sequencing, placemat activities	N/A
explore the layout of web pages to create material using available tools	N/A
revise and improve writing, explaining why they have made changes	An expectation from Standard 4 onwards
Writing: Organising ideas and discussion **Structure and organisation**	
use features which show the structure of the writing, e.g. sub-headings, captions	Standard 6: 1, 18
write an introduction that establishes context, a series of appropriately ordered points and a suitable conclusion	Standard 6: 8
use paragraphs, which have a main idea and related details	Standard 6: 5
use images, graphs and illustrations which are clear, relevant and appropriate	N/A
Writing accurately: language	
use language appropriate to writing, including standard forms of English	Standard 6: 2, 19
use appropriate vocabulary, including subject-specific words and phrases.	Standard 6: 4
Writing accurately: grammar, punctuation, spelling, handwriting	
use different sentence structures, including complex sentences showing relationships of time, or cause, e.g. before you start . . . , if you do this then . . .	Standard 6: 6, 9, 17, 20
use conditionals to show hypotheses or possibilities, e.g. if, might, could	Standard 4: 20
use the full range of punctuation to guide the reader in complex sentences, e.g. commas, bullet points, speech marks and apostrophes for possession	Standard 6: 10, 11, 21
use a variety of strategies to spell words with complex regular patterns, e.g. exercise, competition	Standard 6: 14
produce legible, cursive handwriting with increasing fluency	Standard 6: 12

Oxford Primary Writing Assessment

Year 6

Writing: Organising ideas and discussion Meaning, purposes, readers	Oxford Writing Criterion Scale link
adapt writing style to suit the reader and purpose, *e.g. formal style for unknown reader, simple style for younger readers*	Standard 7: 11, 12, 13, 14, 15
write a comprehensive account of a topic or theme	Standard 7: 20
use a range of strategies to plan writing, *e.g. notes, diagrams, flowcharts*	N/A
explore different ways to present work and use them appropriately, *e.g. moving image, slides, voice over*	N/A
reflect on, edit and redraft to improve their writing	An expectation from Standard 4 onwards
Writing: Organising ideas and discussion Structure and organisation	
adapt structures in writing for different contexts, *e.g. reporting an event, investigation or experiment*	Standard 7: 6
write an effective introduction that establishes context and purpose, a suitable balance between facts and viewpoints, a precise conclusion	Standard 7: 2, 20
use paragraphs making links between them	Standard 7: 6, 7, 9
use features and layout which are constructed to present data and ideas clearly.	Standard 7: 5, 13
Writing accurately: language	
use language appropriate to writing, including standard forms of English	Standard 7: 17, 19
use varied and appropriate vocabulary, including subject-specific words and phrases.	Standard 7: 16
Writing accurately: grammar, punctuation, spelling, handwriting	
use varied sentence structures for emphasis and effect	Standard 7: 8, 10, 18
use the full range of punctuation accurately to clarify meaning	Standard 7: 3
use strategies to spell correctly polysyllabic, complex and irregular words	Standard 7: 1
produce fluent and legible handwriting	Standard 7: 4

The Oxford Writing Criterion Scale and the Northern Ireland Language and Literacy Curriculum

Key Stage 1

Writing expectations	Oxford Writing Criterion Scale links
Understand and use a range of vocabulary by investigating and experimenting with language	At Standard 2: 11, 19
	At Standard 3: 4, 6, 14, 15, 16
	At Standard 4: 5, 15, 17, 18, 19, 20
Begin to check their work in relation to specific criteria	An expectation from Standard 4 onwards
Write without prompting, making their own decisions about form and content	At Standard 1: 7, 11, 14, 16, 19
	At Standard 2: 7, 10, 11, 15, 22
	At Standard 3: 3, 4, 5, 6, 8, 14, 15, 16
	At Standard 4: 1, 3, 4, 11, 13, 19
Write for a variety of purposes and audiences	At Standard 1: 2, 6, 11, 14, 16, 19
	At Standard 2: 1, 7, 10, 11, 15, 22
	At Standard 3: 3, 5, 8,
	At Standard 4: 3, 4, 13, 21
Express thoughts, feelings and opinions in imaginative and factual writing	At Standard 3: 14, 15
	At Standard 4: 13, 17, 19
Understand some of the differences between spoken and written language	At Standard 4: 13
Use a variety of skills to spell words in their writing	At Standard 1: 9, 10, 15, 18
	At Standard 2: 5, 6, 13, 14, 20
	At Standard 3: 10, 11
	At Standard 4: 16
Spell correctly a range of familiar, important and regularly occurring words	At Standard 1: 9, 10, 15, 18
	At Standard 2: 3, 6, 13
	At Standard 3: 10, 11
	At Standard 4: 16
Develop increasing competence in the use of grammar and punctuation	At Standard 2: 12, 16, 18, 21
	At Standard 3: 5, 9, 12, 13, 15, 17, 20
	At Standard 4: 6, 7, 8, 9, 10, 12, 18, 20

Key Stage 2

Writing expectations	Oxford Writing Criterion Scale links
Apply various features of layout as appropriate within their own writing	At Standard 5: 4, 10
	At Standard 6: 1, 5, 13, 18
	At Standard 7: 5, 6, 13
Experiment with rhymes, rhythms, verse structure and all kinds of word play	At Standard 5: 2, 16, 19
	At Standard 6: 19
	At Standard 7: 17
Write for a variety of purposes and audiences, selecting, planning and using appropriate style and form	At Standard 5: 2, 4, 9, 11, 18
	At Standard 6: 2, 3, 8, 13, 17, 18
	At Standard 7: 2, 11, 13, 14
Use the skills of planning, revising and redrafting to improve their writing	An expectation from Standard 4 onwards
Express thoughts, feelings and opinions in imaginative and factual writing	At Standard 5: 1, 8, 11, 18
	At Standard 6: 8, 16, 18, 22
	At Standard 7: 7, 9, 11, 15, 18
Use a variety of stylistic features to create mood and effect	At Standard 5: 16 19
	At Standard 6: 11, 15, 16, 17, 19, 21
	At Standard 7: 2, 5, 16, 17, 18,
Begin to formulate their own personal style	At Standard 5: 19
	At Standard 6: 22
	At Standard 7: 12, 18, 20, 21
Understand the differences between spoken and written language	At Standard 5: 2
	At Standard 6: 2
	At Standard 7: 13, 14
Use a variety of skills to spell words correctly	At Standard 5: 13
	At Standard 6: 14
	At Standard 7: 1
Develop increasing competence in the use of grammar and punctuation to create clarity of meaning	At Standard 5: 4, 5, 7, 8, 9, 10, 12, 14, 15
	At Standard 6: 2, 5, 6, 7, 8, 9, 10, 11, 15, 21
	At Standard 7: 3, 7, 8, 10, 17, 19
Develop a swift and legible style of handwriting	At Standard 5: 6
	At Standard 6: 12, 13
	At Standard 7: 4, 5

Appendix 4: Skills Progression for Big Writing

Schools who follow the *Big Writing* approach, or schools who would prefer to see the strands for writing grouped by individual skill, may wish to use the following skills progression ladders and associated child speak targets rather than the amalgamated 'Grammar and punctuation (including connectives)' strand on pages 62–64. The *Big Writing* Punctuation and Connectives pyramids have been updated in line with National Expectations and are included on pages 141–142.

Punctuation

Name:		Date:	
Year/Key Stage	**Reference Number**	**Small step target / Child speak target (Year 1 onwards)**	**Secure skill? (✔, ✗, ●)**
Reception NB: These targets are not for sharing with the children in this form, but small aspects of a target may be given orally and in a non-stressful way.	P1	Can point to full stops followed by capital letters in other people's writing.	
	P2	Can point to and name full stops and capital letters.	
	P3	Knows that there must always be a capital letter after a full stop.	
	P4	Can put a full stop on the end of a given sentence.	
	P5	Can put full stops into a short piece of writing that is understood.	
	P6	Can find all the full stops in a short piece of writing.	
	P7	Can put missing capital letters after the full stops in a short piece of writing.	
Year 1 From Year 1 onwards, the targets are presented as child-speak targets for sharing with the children.	P8	I am beginning to use full stops and capital letters to show where sentences begin and end in my writing.	
	P9	I know what a question mark looks like.	
	P10	I can use some full stops and capital letters to show most sentences in my writing.	
	P11	I can point to question marks in writing.	
	P12	I can usually use full stops and capital letters to show sentences in my writing.	
	P13	I can tell which sentences are questions.	
	P14	I can change my voice for a question mark in reading.	
	P15	I can draw question marks on the ends of questions.	
	P16	I can point to commas in writing.	
	P17	I always use full stops and capital letters accurately to show sentences in my writing.	
	P18	I am beginning to use questions marks in my writing.	
	P19	I am beginning to use commas in my writing.	
	P20	I can use capital 'I' consistently, to name myself.	
	P21	I use a capital letter to start the word, when writing someone's name.	

Punctuation (cont.)

Name:		Date:	
Year/Key Stage	**Reference Number**	**Small step target / Child speak target (Year 1 onwards)**	**Secure skill? (✔, ✗, ●)**
Year 2	P22	I can usually use question marks in my writing, when they are needed.	
	P23	I can point to and name exclamation marks in writing.	
	P24	I can change my voice for an exclamation mark in reading.	
	P25	I can help to put commas between things in a list in written sentences.	
	P26	I can put exclamation marks on the end of simple exclamations.	
	P27	I can always use full stops, question marks and capitals correctly to show sentences.	
	P28	I can usually use exclamation marks in the right place in my writing.	
	P29	I can point to apostrophes in a piece of writing. *(Singular possession and simple contraction only at Key Stage 1.)*	
	P30	I am beginning to use commas in my writing.	
	P31	I can put commas in the correct places in given sentences.	
	P32	I can use apostrophes *(for singular possession)* in given sentences.	
	P33	I can always use full stops, capital letters, question marks and exclamation marks correctly in my writing.	
	P34	I can usually use commas for lists correctly in my writing.	
	P35	I am beginning to use apostrophes *(for singular possession)* correctly in my writing.	
	P36	I can use apostrophes to show ownership *(e.g. the dog's bone)*.	
	P37	I can use commas correctly for lists in my writing.	
	P38	I can use apostrophes *(for singular possession)* correctly in my writing.	
	P39	I can use apostrophes *(for simple contractions)* in given sentences.	
	P40	I am beginning to use apostrophes for simple contractions correctly in my writing.	
	P41	I can use apostrophes for simple contractions correctly in my writing.	

Punctuation (cont.)

Name:		Date:	
Year/Key Stage	**Reference Number**	**Small step target / Child speak target (Year 1 onwards)**	**Secure skill? (✔, ✗, ●)**
Key Stage 2	P42	I can use all KS1 punctuation accurately (. ! ? , ').	
	P43	I can use commas after fronted adverbials.	
	P44	I can name ellipsis, hyphen, dashes and speech marks correctly. *(May be given each as a separate target)*	
	P45	I can put all the following punctuation into a given piece of writing: . ! ? , ' … -""	
	P46	I can use inverted commas (speech marks) to show direct speech.	
	P47	I can use all the following punctuation in my own writing, mainly accurately: . ! ? , ' … -""	
	P48	I can name brackets, semi-colon and colon correctly. *(This can be further differentiated by targeting each one individually.)*	
	P49	I can accurately punctuate direct speech.	
	P50	I can use a colon to introduce a list.	
	P51	I can use appropriate punctuation to show parenthesis. (() -- , ,)	
	P52	I can use semi colons to mark boundaries between independent clauses.	
	P53	I can use dashes to mark boundaries between independent clauses.	
	P54	I can use colons to mark boundaries between independent clauses.	
	P55	I can use the following range of punctuation in my own writing, mainly accurately, when appropriate: . ! ? , ' … -"" () ; :	
	P56	I can use punctuation for effect or impact.	
	P57	I can use punctuation appropriately for purpose in lists, including the colon and semi-colons.	
	P58	I use the full range of punctuation appropriately and accurately.	

Connectives

Name:		Date:
Year/Key Stage	**Reference Number**	**Small step target / Child speak target (Year 1 onwards)**
Reception NB: These targets are not for sharing with the children in this form, but small aspects of a target may be given orally and in a non-stressful way.	C1	Can point to the word 'and' in short pieces of writing.
	C2	Knows that 'and' is used to join things or simple sentences.
	C3	Can point to 'but' and 'so' in writing. *(May be given individually as separate targets.)*
	C4	Can use 'and', 'but' and 'so' in talk. *(May be given individually as separate targets.)*
	C5	Can use 'and' in own writing.
	C6 (V8)	Can use connectives such as 'and', 'but', 'so' and 'then' in my talk.
Year 1 From Year 1 onwards, the targets are presented as child-speak targets for sharing with the children.	C7	I can use simple sequence words in my writing. *(E.g. First, then, next, last, before, after, etc.)*
	C8	I can use 'and', 'but' and 'so' to join simple sentences.
	C9	I can use a wider range of connectives in my writing. *(E.g. but, so, and, then, etc.)*
	C10	I am trying to use simple linking words and phrases in my writing. *(E.g. after, before, then, soon, at last, etc.)*
	C11	I am trying to use one or two new connectives in my writing. *(E.g. or, if, when, because, as, although, etc.)*
	C12	I can sometimes start a sentence with a connective.
Year 2	C13	I can use a range of connectives in my writing. *(E.g. or, if, when, because, as, although, etc.)*
	C14 (V27)	I can use a wider range of connectives, such as: 'when', 'if', 'because', 'as', 'as well as' and 'although' in my talk and in my writing, when they are needed.
	C15	I can use a range of linking and sequence words. *(E.g. before, after, later, next, also, after a while, at the same time, one day, Last week, etc.)*
	C16	I can use a range of connectives to open sentences in my writing. *(E.g. If… When… Because…)*
	C17	I try not to use the same connective too often.
Key Stage 2	C18	I can use more sophisticated connectives in my writing. *(E.g. although, however, nevertheless, as well as, despite, contrary to, in spite of, etc.)*
	C19	I can use more sophisticated linking and sequencing phrases in my writing. *(E.g. eventually, as a result of, in addition to, in spite of, as well as, a little while later, soon after that, since, etc.)*
	C20	I can use more sophisticated connectives to open sentences in my writing. *(E.g. Although…, However…, Despite…, Contrary to…)*
	C21	I can use sophisticated connectives and links within sentences and to open sentences in my writing. *(E.g. In addition to…, As if…, Nevertheless…, Despite…, Contrary to…, Eventually…, Consequently…, Subsequently…, Referring back to…, In anticipation of…, etc.)*
	C22	I can use a wide range of sophisticated connectives, linking words and sequence words correctly and confidently in my writing.

The Punctuation Pyramid

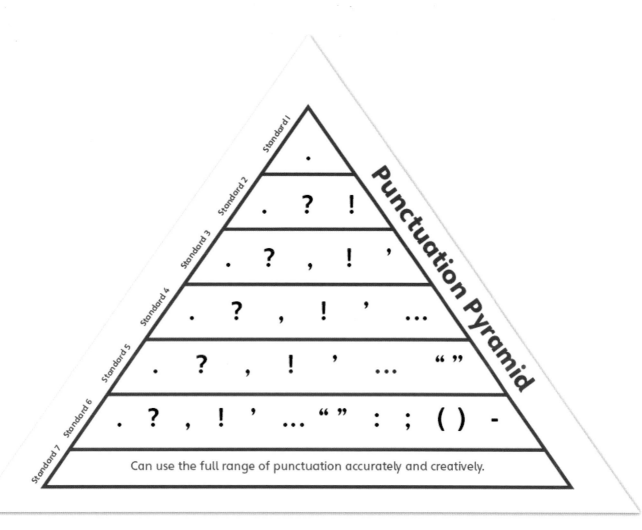

The Connectives Pyramid

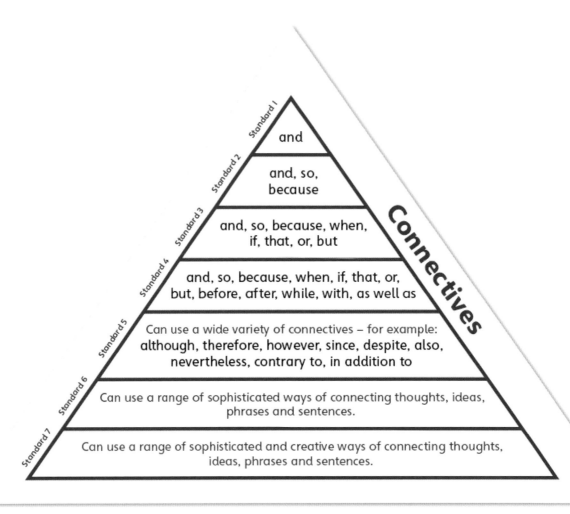

Standard 1 — and

Standard 2 — and, so, because

Standard 3 — and, so, because, when, if, that, or, but

Standard 4 — and, so, because, when, if, that, or, but, before, after, while, with, as well as

Standard 5 — Can use a wide variety of connectives – for example: although, therefore, however, since, despite, also, nevertheless, contrary to, in addition to

Standard 6 — Can use a range of sophisticated ways of connecting thoughts, ideas, phrases and sentences.

Standard 7 — Can use a range of sophisticated and creative ways of connecting thoughts, ideas, phrases and sentences.

Connectives

Notes

Notes